New Texas 2001

Edited by
Donna Walker-Nixon
James Ward Lee

Assistant Editor
Jane Haywood

Editorial Assistant
Carolyn Poulter

Layout and Design
Randy Yandell

Cover Photo
Susan Saunders

Photo Essay
William Scheick

University of Mary Hardin-Baylor
Belton, Texas

A Center for Texas Studies Book

ISBN# 0-9674523-4-1   ISSN# 1522-287X

Board of Advisors

For information, contact:

Donna Walker-Nixon
UMHB Box 8008
900 College Street
Belton, TX 76513
Phone: (254) 295-4564
Email: dwnixon@umhb.edu

Table of Contents

Cleatus Rattan   *Cisco*

GENERATIONS

Days of atonement—we might have been Jewish
except we were Episcopalian.
After Sunday lunch, mother started. She vacuumed
the tops of curtain arcs in rooms with ceilings 12 feet high.
Rooms none entered
unless they were almost strangers, no covenant with them.
Mother polished the glossy tops of tables
no one dared approach. Only she possessed
the secret of survivable touch.

Father paid his price beside the garage
with a chamois skin that could not be made dry.
One drop of holy water always remained.
Squeeze until blood would run
from your hand, there was always another drop.
If one water spot had continued in the Red Sea,
father would not have crossed.

Grandfather did not trust decadent, work-easing cars.
If grandfather had only known
what pleasures lay
in automobiles, he would not have allowed one on his ranch.
Tractors were moral, no pleasure there,
except in some ethic.

After church you were naked, nowhere to hide,
like hungry little children,
shown in grainy black & white pictures,
starving in Europe, pursued by Devils.

Father was relentless in his desire
for my purification by soul-cleansing,
hand-wrinkling, wet work.

Sundays lasted eternally. A sip of wine
transferred father to a higher level
of hellish activity where he could guard against an afternoon nap,
even after the heavy toll had been extracted.

1

Some day my sons will look back on Sundays,
know votive candles in front of blue screens
saved the Cowboys from the relentless pursuit of demons
storming in from Philadelphia, New York, Washington
and other exotic, exile places.
Endless babble
from pundits will tell them
they have been redeemed.

They can relax, watch crops grow,
the sun return, devils depart.

*Winner of the New Texas Poetry Award
given in memory of Dr. Robert H. Woodward by
Dr. Larry and Carol Woodward*

Melissa DeCarlo   *Tyler*

WEEDS

This week, I am collecting relatives and wildflowers at the same rate. The flowers must be uprooted carefully, placed between two pieces of brown paper, to absorb their moisture, and then flattened beneath reference books. When the relatives show up for their annual visit, they arrive on their own, requiring only cheek to cheek air kisses followed by copious refreshments. No plucking or mashing under heavy objects needed, or permitted, unfortunately.

Friday I find a patch of Carolina Jasmine growing in the crack between my fence and my neighbor's, that's close enough to wild for me. I look in my reference book and there it is, *Gelsemium Sempervirens*, its name sounding less like a flower than a rare digestive disorder. That same afternoon my husband's mother's sister's husband arrives. Would that be my uncle-in-law?

I don't need to look up Uncle Jake in any book. I can identify him at first glance: benign, bumbling sixty-year-old, with two chins and an occasional patch of pale skin peeking out from between straining shirt buttons. His fleshy nose is tipped with purple, and his scent—Aqua Velva—trails in his wake, creeping deeper into the house each day, like Kudzu unleashed in a verdant forest.

The following day I find a *Trifolium Repens*, whose ordinary name is White Clover, and a good-sized *Linatia Texans*, a.k.a. Texas Toad Flax. These discoveries mirror the arrival of my husband's brother, William and his wife, Rhonda, a.k.a. Bitsy. Bitsy perches on the edges of chairs, her brows plucked into perfect arches over eyes so caked with mascara that they look like enormous brown spiders. Bitsy eats only salads, drives a red Mary-Kay sedan, and actually irons and starches her hot-pads. She tries to convince me that if I'd just get up earlier, wear lip-liner, and have a pedicure every week, I could really amount to something. She uses herself as an example.

My husband's brother has an easy laugh and still leans back as he sits next to me on the couch. In the three years they have been married, he hasn't completely succumbed to Bitsy, the pod-person.

"William, please get your feet off of the coffee table," Bitsy says, even though my feet are resting on the table right next to his.

Bill and I sneak a sideways glance at each other, and I notice a certain tightness around his eyes that wasn't there last year. Maybe Bitsy has started starching his underwear.

I leave my feet where they are, but Bill lowers his to the floor. Our cat takes this opportunity to leap from my lap to the coffee table, and bat a stray crayon across the smudged glass surface. Bitsy is visibly annoyed but says nothing. I know that she wants to pick up the crayon and tuck it inside its intact box on a neatly arranged shelf in an organized cabinet, but she knows that none of these things can be found in my house. She also wants to tell the cat to get off the table, but fears that the cat, unlike Bill, will ignore her.

The last relative, my husband's sister, arrives at the airport on Monday afternoon. After placing her suitcases—three for a one-week visit—in the trunk, I pull back onto the State Highway 64. A few minutes later I notice a nice patch of Crimson Clover, *Trifolium Incarnatum*, growing on the roadside. Swerving to the shoulder, I leap out, dash to the edge of the road, and grab a handful. For a second I enjoy the warm afternoon sun on my face and the sharp green scent of the clover. Then a semi rushes past, pulling grit and roadside trash in its wake. I straighten and look back at the car. Stella watches me with narrowed eyes.

Five miles later my sister-in-law can take it no longer. "Why did you do that?" she asks, a little too casually.

"Do what?"

"Pull those weeds from the side of the road." She enunciates slowly, as if speaking to a person of very low intellect.

"Because I wish I had a penis," I reply. Stella is a psychologist, and I say this to annoy her. It works. She is blessedly silent the rest of the way home.

Uncle Jake, who was still in bed when I left for the airport, is awake when we arrive. Florid nose abloom, he helps us unload the luggage and carry it to my son's room. Stella frowns at the cowboy bedspread and scattered western paraphernalia.

"These pictures are hung too low," she announces.

"It's a kids room."

"Still..."

I see in her eyes that I must immediately hide my husband's toolbox.

"Your suitcases are awfully heavy. What did you pack?" I ask, fearing that she has brought her own hammer.

"Books. I am working on my dissertation."

"Still?"

I have said the wrong thing again.

She pulls her lips back in a feral smile. "And how about you? Are you still taking those ceramic classes?"

I smile back. "Sculpting classes."

"Oh. I'd love to take a look at some of your efforts."

It's the word "efforts" that makes me say, "I'll have to bring some home from the studio. You know, they're not appropriate to display in a house with small children."

Her eyebrows reach for her box-cut bangs. Ha! Precisely the desired effect. I now must go down and hide the three innocent free-form pieces in the study, then perhaps borrow some of my lesbian friend Maribell's work. My sister-in-law would find me much more interesting if I had some unresolved phallic-worship issues.

This evening at dinner, the atmosphere is strained. Our words seem sharp, our silence heated, stretched thin and brittle like pulled sugar drawn taut across the table.

I'm almost grateful when my seven-year-old whines into a particularly awkward pause, "What are these green specks in the mashed potatoes?"

"Chives."

"Aren't chives the same as onions?"

"They're more like grass clippings." This helpful comment comes from Uncle Jake.

"Gross!"

"I don't know what you're so worried about," says Ryan, my twelve-year-old. "You're always eating your boogers, and they're green. . ."

At this point both of my children erupt in a shouting match made up entirely of the words "shut-up" and "stupid" and "make-me" in no apparent order.

"That's it!" I raise my hands and my voice. "Both of you may be excused."

Ryan stands, belches, and carries his dishes to the sink. Brett starts to do the same, but his knife and fork slide off the plate. Laughing, Ryan kicks the fork, sending it skittering along the linoleum.

"Stop it, jerk!"

"Don't call me a jerk, gay-wad."

Their voices fade, mercifully, with distance.

"What's a gay-wad?" asks Uncle Jake.

My husband flushes and tries to laugh. "Those boys. Who knows why they act the way they do?"

Stella cannot pass up this opportunity to make one of her pompous little analyses. "I think," she leans forward and lowers her voice, "You should keep an eye on Ryan. He may be a just a little homophobic."

"Really?" I say, leaning forward as well. "I think that you may be just a little full-of-shit."

"Excuse me, but I happen have a Master's degree in—"

"How many children do you have."

"None. But I've studied adolescent behavior—"

"How many twelve-year-old boys have you crammed in your car and driven to baseball practice?"

"That's completely beside the point."

"Wrong. It *is* the point."

Stella straightens up and sighs. "I'm sorry, but I think it's obvious to everyone here that you're not a psychiatric authority."

"That's okay. *I* think it's obvious to everyone here that you're a gay-wad." I stand and carry my plate to the sink, gratified to hear a snort of smothered laughter coming from someone at the table.

"Ladies, ladies. . .please. . ." Uncle Jake's nose is almost as dark as the *Erodium Texanum* I found last month. To keep the peace I come back to the table and sit down. We all try to revive the conversation, but it's no use. It's more than just wilted. It's dead.

For the rest of the evening we manage to avoid dangerous topics, and one another whenever possible. At last Uncle Jake, then my children, and finally my husband drift off to bed. But still I do not have the house to myself. The two people I most wish were sleeping are still awake.

It is after midnight when I ease open my bedroom door and check on the boys. Sprawled across pallets on the floor, they are no longer calling each other names, instead they fill the room with quiet rustlings and sighs, and the faint scent of soap and damp hair.

I turn and find Bitsy standing behind me.

"Sometimes I wish. . ." She lets the words drift off and watches my children with hungry eyes.

"You could adopt."

She shakes her head. "I would worry about where they came from, who they would be."

"Then you'd be no different from any other mother."

I walk to the dining room and Bitsy follows me. As we pass through the living room, Stella looks up from her reading. Out of the corner of my eye, I see her stand and follow us.

Stopping at the dining room table, I lift *Webster's Unabridged*, and press my hand against the damp paper underneath.

Stella draws close and says, "I'm sorry about what happened at dinner."

"Hand me a piece of that brown paper sack."

Bitsy tears off a piece and hands it to Stella who then hands it to me.

"I don't really think there's anything wrong with Ryan."

I take the paper from her hand. "I'm sorry too. I don't really think you're a gay-wad."

I watch her reflection in the darkened window and I think I see her smile.

As I carefully transfer the limp bloom onto the fresh paper, Stella asks, "Are you ready to tell me why you're doing this?"

I consider goading her some more, but it's late. I'm tired. "It's Ryan's science project. I've gotten most of it done, but I still need nine more flowers."

"Why isn't Ryan doing this?" Stella asks.

"He lost interest about twenty flowers ago." I press another dry piece of paper on top of the blossom and place the heavy book on top.

Stella puts her hand on my shoulder. "Well, I guess now you know."

"Know what?"

"Why ferrets eat their young."

The three of us laugh and for once I'm not annoyed that Bitsy's teeth are marked with lipstick. And although Stella's hand feels too warm on my shoulder, I leave it there.

Bitsy turns away and opens the shoebox that contains the flowers I collected last fall, now pressed and mounted on 4X6 index cards. Stella and I watch over her shoulder as she shuffles through them. It's funny how the colors haven't faded, they've deepened, become more than what they were. The whites are now yellow, the yellows are brownish-orange, the reds and blues have turned a deep blister-purple.

Bitsy pulls out a card laminated with a sprig of henbit and another with a dandelion. "But these are just weeds."

"Depends on your perspective," I say.

"That's right." Stella catches my eye and grins. "Some people just pull weeds. Others gather wildflowers."

Bitsy pauses, then carefully sets the *Lamium Amplexicaule* and the *Teraxcum Officianale* back in the box. "I guess I never thought about it that way before."

I look at Bitsy and Stella, and I smile, really seeing them perhaps for the first time. And then for a second, a heartbeat, I find myself wanting to preserve this moment—wishing that I could gather these two women in my arms, and press them against me.

Yvette Roshelleye Blair   *Dallas*

FUDGE BOMBS AND CRACKER JACKS

"You might not ever been rich, but lemme tell you it's better than digging a ditch. Ain't no tellin' who you might see. A movie star or maybe even a...working at the car wash. Whoa, whoa, whoa, whoa, talking about the car wash.."

Every time Serita heard that song blaring from the ice cream truck down the street, she ran to her mama, tugged on her dress and asked for the fifty cents to get her a fudge bomb.

"Mama, can I pleeease have two quarters to get me a fudge bomb?" Serita's voice would trail off like a whistling train going down the track.

" What'd you do with the fifty cents I gave you yesterday, Serita," her mama asked sternly, looking down at Serita for an answer.

"I bought a box of cracker jacks with it, Mama," Serita said coyly, adding the term of endearment hoping to sway her mother into giving her the ice cream money.

"Girl, I swear, between you getting those fudge bombs and those box of cracker jacks, you gon' eat your way to junk food kingdom. You can buy ice cream today, but don't come in here tomorrow asking me for no more money to buy no junk food. You hear me?"

Serita heard her. She also heard her all the other times she had said that same thing.

Serita grabbed the two shiny quarters and darted out the back door. As she was waiting for the ice cream truck to pull up in front of her house, she spotted Kashanda coming down the sidewalk with her older sister, La Toya. Kashanda was in the fourth grade like Serita, but she was a year older because her birthday came in September and her mother waited until Kashanda was seven before she entered her in the first grade. And her sister, La Toya, was in seventh grade already. She was 13-years-old.

Serita walked back up to her porch and held onto the doorknob, twisting it, as she saw Kashanda and La Toya heading closer toward the ice cream truck.

"Cry baby, cry baby, suck your mama's —," Kashanda had started when she noticed that Serita's mother had come onto the porch.

Serita was glad that her mother came to the rescue. Again. Ever since Serita and Kashanda got into that fight over bumping into each other on the sidewalk when they were both hoola-hooping, Serita was admittedly scared of Kashanda. Plus when La Toya came out and saw the two girls in a shoving match, and what looked like Serita was winning, she pushed Serita down into the grass.

La Toya got in trouble for it, but she still scared Serita just the same. And ever since then, Serita made certain that she wasn't outside alone with the sights of those two near.

"Come on baby and let's get your fudge bomb. I think I'll get one for

Devaughn. He likes those, too," Serita's mama said as she took her by the hand and headed toward the ice cream truck.

Serita looked over at Kashanda and La Toya. Kashanda was eyeing her and mimicking the rest of the sentence that she started when Serita's mama came out. She rushed to get ahead of Serita, hoping to get the last fudge bomb before Serita did. Just as she was about to get to the ice cream truck, she tripped on her Lemon Twist that was on the sidewalk. La Toya ran toward her crying sister to help her up. Kashanda had gravel all in her hair. She was so embarrassed. She got up, crying, and ran back home. After that incident, Serita didn't need her mother to go with her to the ice cream truck.

* * *

The ice cream man had turned the music up louder, hoping that more kids from Arpege Circle would come out and buy ice cream, candy or pickles. This was the same ice cream man that had been coming on their street since Serita was in kindergarten. And one time when Serita only had enough to buy one fudge bomb and a little chick-o-stick instead of the bigger one, the ice cream man gave it to her anyway. He was nice and all the kids in the neighborhood liked him. Plus, they liked that he always had the pop rock candy that their parents wouldn't buy them in the grocery stores.

The bigger kids, the ones who were in the eighth grade, would buy the pop rock candy and all the little kids would stand around and listen as the candy sizzled and popped in the bigger kids' mouths. All the boys in the neighborhood, the ones from Ryan Road, O'Bannon Street and Hoke Smith, would stand around and have pop rock-eating contests. That is, all the boys except Alvin.

Alvin, a sissy boy, who lived straight in the middle of the circle with his mama, and two older sisters, was very neat and particular about himself. He didn't play stickball or pop wheelies on his bike like the other boys he did. In fact, Alvin rode a girl's bike. It was a pink Huffy bike with a basket in front and a little horn on the left handle bar. Whenever the wind was blowing real hard, you could see those pink and white streamers on the handlebars dancing in the wind.

Since Alvin had two sisters, his mother figured there was no need in buying a bike for Alvin. The bike that his sisters rode was in perfect condition, save for the broken light reflector on the back wheel. Alvin rode that bike with pride. All the kids on the street would tease him and run after Alvin screaming, *"sissy boy, sissy boy, riding on a girl's toy."*

Alvin always had Now-&-Laters (sour apple ones and the banana ones), Bubblicious bubble gum and Coconut Boys candies in his basket. Plus he always had a box of Cracker Jacks. One time he had gotten a Super Sleuth Magnifying Glass from inside. It was the same kind that Ricochet Rabbit on the afternoon cartoons used to solve mysteries.

Alvin was real proud of it, too.

Sometimes the eighth-graders from over on Hoke Smith would catch Alvin as he was riding down the sidewalk on that pink Huffy bike and knock him down. All of those Now-&-Laters and Coconut Boys would get smashed in the ground underneath the bike's tire. The boys would salvage what they could of the bubble gum.

That Super Sleuth Magnifying Glass never had a chance. Broken bits of it were sprawled along the sidewalk.

"He ain't nuthin' but a ol' faggot anyway. Look at him. Eating girl's candy. He too scaredy to eat pop rocks. Thirteen years old and still eating those little Coconut Boys. Look at him. He probably done peed in his panties," laughed Darrin, the boy that La Toya liked.

Alvin was always getting picked on by somebody. Especially the time that he wore that pink shirt with the ruffles at the end of the sleeves. He had just left the ice cream truck and was walking down the street eating his fudge bomb. Just as he was nearing his house, the boys came up through the alley. They were playing with a Frisbee and threw it at Alvin. It hit him right in the back of the head. He lost his balance and fell. When he got up, the fudge bomb was all over him.

Alvin never fought back. Not because he was a sissy, but because he was a little preacher. Alvin's grandmother was on the motherboard at church and she always made Alvin go with her. Church on Sundays, church on Monday nights for the motherboard meetings and Church on Wednesdays for Bible Study.

One Monday night at motherboard meeting, Alvin's grandmother made him get up and give the prayer. He read from the 131st Psalm. When he finished, the women were fascinated by the way that he said, *"may the Lord add a blessing to the readers, hearers and doers of His holy word. Aaaa-man!"*

They told Miss Earline that Alvin had all the makings of a little preacher. Alvin's grandmother was so proud that she saved up her S&H Green Stamps to get him a Bible.

Alvin was really into that stuff. He led the prayers on Monday nights and he even had a chance to share the word on Wednesday nights at Bible study. In fact, he was so into it that he even went so far as to try and get the ice cream man to put gospel music in the ice cream truck so that the kids could hear *"This little light of mine I'm gon' let it shine...ohhh, this little light of mine."*

***

All of that teasing and messing with Alvin went on for most of the school year 'til finally one day something happened.

One afternoon, the ice cream truck came just as everybody was walking home from school. Alvin raced up to the ice cream truck, running like a girl, while the boys made cooing sounds at him and called him a faggot.

"Hey Alvin, they probably all out of fudge bombs. I think Serita got the last one," hollered Darrin.

"Yea, all they have left is pop rock candy...you know the candy that boys eat," Nelda chided in.

Alvin was determined to show them that he was "boy enough" to eat that pop rock candy. And to prove it, he was going to get the raspberry-flavored kind. This one was the flavor that the more experienced kids bought because the combination of the tart taste with the sizzling and popping could cause you to choke.

Darrin, Nelda, and Bobby Junior had already laid their money up on the counter for two pickles, a Big Red pop and a bag of Andy's Hot Fries. And just as they were about to leave with their stash, Nelda turned back and put seventy-five cents on the counter and asked the man for three packets of the raspberry-flavored pop rock candy.

"*Man, I almost forgot the pop rock. I'm glad you remembered it because I have a new trick I wanna show y'all,*" said Darrin.

"*I didn't get this for us,*" Nelda exclaimed, looking over at Alvin. "*I got this to see if today is the day we find out whether Alvin is cut out to be a man.*"

All the other kids who were at the ice cream truck got their goodies and headed over to the crowd that was gathering. Nelda and them had cornered Alvin and they were daring him to chug down on the candy.

Darrin, Nelda and Bobby Junior were egging him on. "*He run like a girl, he dress like a girl and he probably eat like a girl,*" said Nelda, the tallest of three boys who was 15 and still in the eighth grade because he had flunked twice. "*He ain't no real boy. He can't eat no pop rock,*" he touted.

Bobby Junior chimed in and told the crowd that had gathered around, that his baby brother could eat a whole pack of raspberry-flavored pop rocks without stopping.

Alvin opened up the first packet and tilted his head back and poured the pop rocks in his mouth. He held out his tongue while everybody stood around and listened to the sizzling and popping sounds.

"*Man, that ain't nothing, I told you my baby brother can eat a pack of pop rocks and he ain't nuthin' but six years old,*" Bobby Junior said, as he started shouting, "*sissy boy*" and getting the crowd of kids to join in.

Just as Alvin was about to open up another packet, his sister, Treneesha, came running up, waving her arms and yelling at Alvin.

Alvin poured in another packet anyway. He tried to swallow the pop rocks this time, but the tart taste caused him to start coughing. Then he started choking.

"*Man, I ain't never seen nobody eat two packets of them at one time,*" Darrin said, backing away from his place up front in the crowd.

Alvin was heaving and gasping for breath. "*Somebody do something,*" his sister shouted, almost in tears.

The ice cream man, who was still there, restocking the pickle jar, saw what was happening and ran out of the truck to help. He grabbed Alvin from behind and started lunging into him. He jolted Alvin a few more times and Alvin fell limp in the ice cream man's arms.

The ice cream man opened up Alvin's mouth. Alvin came to and sat up. His eyes were all red and tears were everywhere.

"*Ahh, look at him. Crying like a girl. I told y'all he ain't nuthin' but a faggot,*" Nelda said, laughing and pointing at Alvin, while eating the last of his Andy's Hot Fries.

11

Nelda leaned over closer to Alvin and got in his face and started making baby sounds. Before anybody knew it, Alvin had socked Nelda in the eye and knocked him to the ground.

"Man that's one of them Bruce Lee moves," one of the kids in the crowd shouted.

After that, nobody called Alvin sissy boy again. Not even when he wore that white blouse to take his school pictures.

Lianne Elizabeth Mercer   *Fredericksburg*

INTERRUPTED LIFE

on learning a friend has Alzheimer's

red and yellow leaves laugh
like painted lovers
invite me to the party of the year
winding down

no cake   just the crisp crunch
of leaves   nothing lasts
ants lick crumbs of relationships
winter is in the air

the kid in me opens her mouth
to catch first snowflakes
cold realities   snow angels
winter games   fox and geese

my heart traverses the seasons
mimicking flames
smoke crawls into gray sky
nothing sings like a dying fire

Robert Fink   *Abilene*

THE DEAD

They are with him always,
tapping outside the window, 5:00 a.m.
as he eases into his cushioned swivel chair
and opens the Laboratory Research Notebook,
200 sheets sewn at the spine.
They enter one by one. Their fingers
caress his cheek. "Now today, my love, ... "
Embracing his shoulders, each leans
over the page: translucent flesh,
bone sifting through a sieve.
He prints their stories
across the graph-paper squares—
a thousand openings he falls into,
is lifted up with each soul rising.

The first three arrived after the tornado.
He was seven, in the back seat
of his father's Buick returning home.
Just inside the city limits, north of what
come morning would not be recognizable,
the car was lifted on God's finger, spun
like a merry-go-round of painted horses
whirling so fast their wooden lips flare back.
His father clutched the steering wheel.
His mother could not scream.
The Buick landed right-side up.

He was seven. First day back at school,
watching janitors remove three classmates'
empty desks, he memorized, before they closed,
the openings in each row.

Lawrence Baines   *Lubbock*

Benchmarks

At different points in my life, my big brother Adam has been my hero, protector, and patron saint. He taught me how to fight, how to focus, and most importantly — how to live like you mean it. When Adam's 40th birthday came around, I wanted to buy him something that somehow communicated all that he had meant to me.

"You could get me some slippers," Adam tells me.

"Slippers? You'd wear slippers?" I ask.

When his wife couldn't think of anything else to complain about, I'm sure she suggested he needed a pair. A cute, melancholy princess, his wife has a penchant for rolling her eyes whenever she gets bored or angry. For the past few months, her eyes have gone completely spastic.

The princess treats Adam as if he were some pesky, old fart. And I can't get over the paradox. My brother, the original Sky Pilot, soaring through the clouds like a god, breaking the hearts of all those prom queens, creating miracles out of the sheer force of his will. With a wife who only sees a graying, tedious, 40-year-old man.

"You know, those furry teddy slippers are really cute," the princess says.

Adam at 10

On my way home from school one day, two seventh grade bullies tackle me, a frail third-grader, off my bicycle. I land face first on the cement and they blitz away with my bike. I run home, crying and bloody, and tell Adam. As I describe the thugs–huge, gnarly, demonic—Adam listens in silence. Then he goes into the garage, grabs a crowbar, and murmurs, "I know who they are and I think I know where they live." He begins walking down the middle of the street, crowbar swinging at his side.

"Forget about the stupid bike! Forget about it! Come back Adam," I scream.

Adam turns and looks at me, smiles a little maniacal smile, slaps the crowbar against his leg, and winks.

I whisper a delirious prayer, "Bring Adam back, God. Bring Adam back," over and over.

In half an hour, I see him on the horizon pedaling slowly towards me, guiding my bike with one hand, holding the crowbar with the other. As he gets closer, I can see that his shirt has been ripped open, one eye trickles blood. He rides the bicycle right up to where I am standing, hops off, places my fingers on the handlebars, and walks away. Doesn't say a word.

Adam at 14

We are watching the old Monkees television show at the house of Big Johnny Lee, a guy from school Adam has started hanging out with. Big John isn't only the most massive guy in ninth grade, he also has the rep as being one of the toughest guys around. Rumor had it that he beat up a senior so bad that the poor kid had to be hospitalized for a couple weeks.

Anyway, just when Monkee Davy Jones is about to break into a sappy love song, Big John rises from his chair and proclaims, "I'm sick of this wimpy show. I want to watch wrestling."

Adam points to me, lying on the floor in front of the television and says, "The kid seems to be enjoying the Monkees right now, Big John." Although I could care less about watching Davy Jones lip-synch, I keep my mouth shut.

Big John says, "You're in my house. It's my TV! "

Then, he says, "punk" under his breath, shoves me aside with one big foot, and grabs the remote control sitting on a pillow next to me. He punches the remote until he finds what he wants—one of those stupid, fake wrestling matches—a bunch of muscle-bound freaks in tight shorts strutting around and bowing up to each other. When Big John sits back down, he places the remote control on the arm of his chair. Adam strides over, swoops it up, and switches the channel back to the Monkees.

John leaps to his feet, unfastens his belt, wraps the brown leather around his fist and says, "You want some of this? Is that it? You put it back on wrestling or I'll bust your head open." Spit oozes from the corners of Big John's mouth and rolls down his chin. He taps the belt buckle with a finger, glowers at me, and when he jerks around to face Adam, the spit goes flying.

Adam turns the channel back to wrestling, pauses, then moves over to the television, where he quickly unscrews the little vertical hold knob at the front of the set. I can hear the wrestlers scream at each other as the picture on the television begins turning fast circles.

"What the hell do you think you're doing? Big John is really yelling now, the fist with the protruding belt buckle hovering over Adam's head. Adam puts the little vertical hold knob in his mouth and swallows.

Adam at 16

The family goes on a grueling road trip to the Grand Canyon. When we arrive at the South Rim for a guided tour, Adam bolts, jumps over the guard ropes, and leaps onto a rock teetering on the edge of the canyon—the bottom a couple thousand feet straight down. Mom shouts, "Oh my God! Adam, what are you doing?"

Dad panics, "Help! Help! My boy!" The ranger stops talking and everyone in the tour group turns and looks in silence at Adam in the forbidden zone on the other side of the ropes, on tiptoes peering over the edge of the canyon. For a moment, I think Adam has jumped and I imagine him in mid-air there glorious, fearless, laughing.

But, Adam is still standing on the edge. Slowly, he raises both arms over his head like a bird preparing his wings for flight, then closes his eyes and pumps both fists in the air.

Adam at 18

Adam earns the nickname Sky Pilot because he is the captain of the track team and the guy with the best vertical jump in school. Although he's only 6'2", he sets a new record for the high jump, and is the only guy on the basketball team who can jump high enough to slam dunk. He scores 24 points in the state basketball championship game, including 8 points on dunks, but the team loses after he fouls out. As time elapses and with Adam relegated to

16

the bench, the crowd chants, "Sky, Sky, Sky, Sky, Sky."

Gradually, I become recognized as Sky Pilot's little brother. Instead of life as a goofy 13-year-old nobody, I hear stuff like, "That's Sky's little brother over there, isn't he cute?" from luscious high school girls I've never even met. And the girls come in waves, all frantic to get a look at the lighting in the eyes of the legendary Sky Pilot.

One cold night during Christmas break, I awaken to tapping on Adam's bedroom window. I walk into the dark room just as he is helping Melissa Holder, the Venus, dream babe, and homecoming queen of Lakeview High School, crawl through. Once in, she motions Adam away, unties her trenchcoat, and lets it slip gently off her shoulders to the ground. Underneath, she's completely naked. Adam laughs softly, but I gasp like a geek, standing in the doorway.

Melissa finally notices me, folds her arms over her breasts, falls to her knees and stammers, "God, God, God," real fast. Adam winks at me and says, "Hey, don't worry about it, baby. He's cool. My little brother is cool."

Adam at 21

Adam begins to develop an appetite for wild-eyed, party girls and discards the sensitive, sane women in his fan club like so much junk mail. Regardless of personality, he only goes out with the Barbie type, girls with perfect bodies and clear complexions who would rather break an arm than get the hair messed up.

At home one weekend from college, Adam borrows dad's new hot red Mustang Mach I to pick up Jennifer Beddington, a particularly fetching Barbie, so that they can go cruising. In Adam's mind, cruising means a drive out to a deserted country road where he and Jennifer would be undisturbed if they decided to spread a blanket on the ground and get naked.

On the way out of town, Adam manages to get the Mustang up to ninety on one of the narrow residential streets before he swerves to miss a kid's soccer ball that rolls in front of the car. The Mustang runs over a fence and levels a brick garden wall before it begins to roll. Jennifer winds up with a little bruise on her forehead, but Adam gets pinned under the dashboard, metal ripping into his legs. When help arrives, firemen have to saw off the roof of the Mustang and pry his body out. By the time they finally get him untangled, Adam's almost dead.

Adam at 25

It takes Adam a couple years to finish rehab. He doesn't talk much, spends extended hours sitting in a lounge chair in the backyard staring at the sky. Mom and dad think he might be going crazy. After a lengthy campaign by friends and family to bring him back into the routine of life, Adam decides to finish his college degree. At school, he changes his major from sculpture to accounting. He launches an earnest campaign to please women and live the wholesome life.

"I just want something that's going to last," he says. Adam attempts to transform himself into a nice guy.

Jan Epton Seale   *McAllen*

SIXTY-SEVENTH ANNIVERSARY

Their love runs deep and down.
Scowls, words pitched like pond stones,
blaming silences all mitigated

By love: loud goodnight smacks,
caresses designed to steady,
parade of coffee, roll call of dead friends.

He says it's good he doesn't own a gun.
She says she won't last to her birthday.
Putting on their shoes takes all morning.

"Go on now," she says, prodding him
when he sticks like a cat in the doorway,
leftover control twitching in his face.

"Your mother doesn't have any idea
at all what's become of her purse," he rats.
"I have to watch her constantly."

They keep switching canes, like relay runners.
"Why not mark them?" a daughter tries.
"Heavens, no!" they bawl in unison.

"Nothing like that..." the old woman starts,
"...makes the slightest bit of difference," he finishes.

Zetta Wiley   ***Fort Worth***

PHOTOGRAPHIC MEMORY

You're not going to believe this, but it's us women who hold things together. Hell, girl, I'd forgotten about that snapshot you're holding. Where'd
you find it? Your grandma's trunk. Should've known. Mama was never one to
throw out nothing.

Let's see here . . . that's the old St. James CME Church. That's your Grandma
Faye and her sister, Aunt Daisy. Yep, that's your mama, Josie, they're helping
down the steps. Lord, I ain't' seen a body look so wretched in my life. You can
tell it's a funeral…see the hearse off to the left?

Mmm, it was the summer of 1940 and it was *hot*. Aunt Daisy's garden didn't
produce nothing but dirt—Stop rolling your eyes, child! It ain't every day my
niece comes to visit and asks, 'Aunt Cassie, is it true my mama killed somebody?' Hell…the person doing the asking owes the other person a minute or
two to think of an answer.

Let me ask you. Do *you* have good girlfriends? A good girlfriend is like your
best girdle. A body can't have too much support.

Anyway, my Mama was out of town when all of this happened. Good thing,
too. Mama was a mean old bitch. She preached about Christian charity, but it
was your mother, Josie, who practiced it—even after what happened.

Now, Aunt Daisy was the total opposite of Mama. Aunt Daisy could have a
good time. She's the one who taught me and Josie how to use eyeliner on the
back of our legs to look like we wore stockings—she also taught us how
Vaseline got it off quick before Mama saw.

Let's see, that photo was took in June 1940, so I was 12, and Josie was 15.
She had started dating Booker John despite Mama's fussing. Booker was nothing but a small time gangster who made bets and tended the Wolf Pack Bar. He
and Aunt Daisy were both 20 and he wanted Daisy bad. Poor Josie. She didn't
know Booker was using her.

But Aunt Daisy had Jimmy Parmenter. Yes, girl, I said *Parmenter* as in the
Big House Parmenters. You had Parmenters running the city council, the
sheriff's department—everything. You couldn't spit in this town without hitting a Negro or a Parmenter.

A white man with a Negro mistress ain't new in the South—just dangerous.
But Daisy and Jimmy didn't care. They loved each other and there wasn't
nothing Jimmy wouldn't do for Aunt Daisy. He proved it, too.

Josie and Booker started dating in the spring, and by summer, Josie was
putting on weight…if you know what I mean.

Well, one evening I was sitting on the couch looking at patterns and listening to Fletcher Henderson when Josie comes storming through the screen
door looking like she'd been fighting. She ran upstairs and slammed our bed-

room door just as Aunt Daisy walked in from her canasta evening.

"What was that?" she asked. "That was Josie," I said and Aunt Daisy went upstairs.

I tiptoed to the stairwell to hear Josie all hysterical saying, "How could he do this? How could I *let* him do it?" Then Aunt Daisy yelled, "He picked the *wrong* family to mess with!"

The sound of feet inside the room told me to get my butt back on the couch. A few minutes later Aunt Daisy came in and said, "Cassie, how would you like to spend the night with Aunt Frankie and Cousin Lola?"

Now, I ain't stupid. Something was going down and I wasn't invited. Besides, Aunt Daisy had my overnight bag in her hand. But I didn't mind going to Aunt Frankie's. She was always in bed by 9:00 and me and Cousin Lola would sneak out the window and hit the streets. Which is exactly what we did.

We strolled down Patterson Street where the moonlight came through the leaves of the giant oaks and willows making the shadows all lacy-like. The moon looked like a honeydew melon and the air smelled just as sweet. As we walked, I fed Lola the latest on Josie and Booker. She ate it up.

"Cassie, don't tell me Josie got *pregnant*," she say.

"*Been* pregnant," I say. "And now Booker's done something stupid. But Aunt Daisy's gonna fix it."

By 2:00, the drunks and hookers were going home and we thought we'd do the same when we found ourselves on Main Street not far from the Wolf Pack Bar.

I saw Jimmy Parmenter's '39 Studebaker Commander parked on the corner. Inside were three people. I could tell Jimmy was behind the wheel because of the fedora he always wore. We got closer and saw two women in his car! Lola and I started laughing because we knew Aunt Daisy would beat the *white* off Jimmy and risk getting lynched if she thought he was with someone else. But we came to realize she *was* in the car.

The third person we didn't see until we were almost on top of them so we ducked into the doorway of the hardware store.

It was Josie sitting in the backseat and never did I see her look so mean. Almost like Mama. But Josie's right eye was swollen and looked the color of eggplant. Her lip was cut, too. We only saw her profile, but that was enough. Booker John had more nerve than a lone Negro heckling at a Klan rally if he thought he could raise a hand to a woman in *my* family.

Booker staggered out of the Wolf Pack and didn't notice the Studebaker start to cruise after him. Lola and I got out of our hiding place. They weren't paying attention to us.

The Studebaker slid around the corner as Booker went down the alley between the library and Tricky's Pawn Shop. Instead of going to the corner, Lola and I cut down the alley next to the Wolf Pack because all alleys emptied at the loading docks of Goodson's Grocery. By the time we got there, all Hell was about to break loose.

Two light bulbs hanging over the loading docks cast a large circle of light.

Girl, we were so close, I could smell the whiskey on Booker's breath.

He came into the light from one end of the alley when Josie and Aunt Daisy appeared at the opposite end. I didn't see Jimmy Parmenter at all.

Josie's pale dress looked dirty, like someone splattered mud on it. I found out later that it was her blood. Daisy was still in her canasta clothes—a dark suit with a lace collar, hat and gloves. But child, they looked *fierce*.

"Booker!" Josie called out.

"Josie?" He yelled back. "Josie, is that you? Dammit, bitch I—"

That was all he got out. Aunt Daisy reached into her purse and took out her revolver. Josie pulled a gun out of her bodice. They didn't give Booker a chance to get the .44 he always carried.

Aunt Daisy shot first and clipped the son of a bitch's right ear—she always did have weak eyes. Booker screamed like a woman and Josie opened fire. I don't know who got him in the head...but Booker's processed hair flew back like it was in a high wind taking a good piece of his scalp with it.

Lola and I held onto each other for everything we was worth. Ooh, child! To my dying day I'll never forget the looks on their faces. Booker's body wriggled and bucked on the ground like spit on a skillet, his blood ran towards Josie's feet and she stepped aside as cool as you please.

When it was over, Jimmy Parmenter came out of the shadows and put his arm around Josie to help her to the car. Aunt Daisy went in for a closer look. She glanced in our direction, saw us, and frowned. She gave us a look as if to say, "You didn't see what you *think* you saw."

She had a gun. Who was we to argue?

But Mama made Josie pay for her sins. When no one would claim Booker, Mama made Josie go to the funeral home to dress him. Then she took Josie to see Miss Gladys to handle Josie's *other* problem...if you know what I mean. You can imagine my surprise when years later Josie wrote to say she was carrying you.

Which brings me back to the picture. Mama made me shoot it—and do you know why? Mama wanted Josie to remember what she'd done so she hung that photo at the foot of Josie's bed so it would be the first and last thing she'd see every day. Ain't no wonder Josie ran away and never came back.

But I don't care what nobody says. I love my sister and my aunt....Besides, Aunt Daisy's the only woman I know who'd wear a hat and gloves to kill a man.

Carol Coffee Reposa   *San Antonio*

ON CHARLES WHITMAN

August 1 was hazy.
Students ambled to their classes
In unwilling herds, books
Balanced on their hips.

Three blocks away
In our decrepit rooms
I struggled with a birthday cake
Butter icing melting in the heat.

Inside the Tower
Carrels bulged with sluggish grads.
Traffic inched in lazy ribbons
Down the Drag.

No one saw
The ex-Marine
Who took the elevator
Far as it would go.

Summer oozed through walls
Crept up furniture.
I put the cake
Inside the fridge.

He reached the observation deck
Unpacked deodorant and rifles
Ate some lunch.
No one saw

At first
The lazy puffs of smoke, or heard
Those dull reports
That sounded like a distant fireworks show.

No one made connection
Even when the passersby
Began to melt
Along the sidewalks

Or in front of cars
And smoke kept rising
From the Tower
In languid spirals

Almost festive, like the fumes
From blown-out candles
On a youngster's
Birthday cake.

They got it, finally.
Phones went off
In high electric screams
And sirens scattered noon.

Police cars raced
Along the streets
In frenzied lines
Like worker ants defending hills

Smashed by a giant mower.
I got a call
From someone penned
Inside the Co-op.

He told me
To take cover
Told me
What I knew.

By nightfall
Heat had drained the campus
As the moon rose indolent
Above the blistered trees.

The cake
Had hardened in the fridge
Too stiff, too cold
To touch.

Michael Bracken   *Waco*

DEAD AIR DAYS

Triple-digit dry heat, no breeze. I leaned against a barren pecan tree and watched the horizon shimmer, heat waves rising off the parched ground. A train whistled two miles off and in the heat I saw my father's ghosts.

I wore a sweat-stained gimme cap, a long-billed baseball hat emblazoned with the logo of a now-defunct granary. I'd tucked my kerchief under the back of the cap, letting it hang over my neck where sweat glued it to my skin. A brand new green-and-gold t-shirt clung to my chest and back, half-moons of sweat darkening my underarms. I wore it tucked into a tight-fitting pair of faded Levi's and my battered Ropers—low-heeled cowboy boots—had long ago molded themselves to the shapes of my feet.

My father had once sat in this same spot, a deer rifle cradled in his hands, the butt of the rifle slamming against his shoulder each time he squeezed the trigger.

"I got three, maybe four of them myself," he'd told me once. I'd just turned twelve, the same age he'd been, and we were in the barn changing the oil in his '59 Chevrolet Apache. "They came running at us, a whole line of them, men, women, and children. We just picked them off like ducks at the shooting gallery."

The Apache sat twenty or thirty feet behind me now, too far away for me to return to the cooler of Lonestar I'd left in the bed. I opened the one bottle I'd carried up the rise with me and took a quick swallow.

That afternoon in the barn, my father lifted the tooled leather patch from his left eye, showing me the blind orb beneath. "Everything ended when Sammy Ledbetter's Winchester kicked out a hot shell."

Ledbetter had been standing to my father's left, sighting down the v-notch of his rifle and taking down two for every one of my father's.

"Kept me out of the war, though," my father said as he fitted the patch back into place. "Got to be grateful for that."

I squinted against the harsh midday sun, counting the first dozen coming into view.

"I still see them, sometimes," my father said years later, after mother had passed and we found ourselves alone in the kitchen with a six pack of Lonestar and a window air conditioner that struggled in vain to push tepid air around the room. "On dead air days like today."

They could have been farm workers or college professors and it wouldn't have made any difference to the men gathered that day. During the Great Depression, Immigration officials packed more than 400,000 men, women, and children into sealed boxcars and shipped them southward toward the border, leaving behind whatever possessions they could not carry. Dust storms had destroyed crops throughout the midwest and god-fearing Christian farmers now lived in the shanties and worked the fields they had once willingly relinquished to brown-skinned foreigners.

The men with my father had each paid twenty dollars to stand on the rise by the pecan tree, money that had been passed from Postmaster Wilson to a pair of Immigration officials riding with the train.

"I had my first beer that day," my father explained. "Woody brought a washtub filled with ice and beer and your granddad pulled one out for each of us. I can still see the flecks of ice glittering on the bottles and the water dripping from his hand."

My father drank that first beer, foam sliding down his chin and his chest, and he'd mopped his forehead with an old undershirt, waiting and listening to granddad and the other men laugh at jokes he'd been too young to understand.

"Smitty spotted the first one rising from the heat," my father explained. "Your granddad sat me down against the tree and told me not to fire until the others started. It seemed like we waited a long time."

My father passed two summers ago and we laid him to rest up in Crawfordsville, next to mother. After Sammy Ledbetter's errant shell had half-blinded my father, granddad had not returned to the shoot. A few years later the United States entered World War II and the men who weren't drafted were no longer available.

Three days after we buried my father, the temperature soared to 112 and heat rose from the ground in waves. I'd been in the back field repairing a break in the fence when I thought I saw someone approaching from over the horizon. I straightened and lifted my hat, mopping my forehead with the back of my arm. Just as I lifted my hand to wave to the oncoming stranger, he dropped from view.

I blinked against the heat, scanning the horizon to see where he'd gone. When the stranger didn't reappear, I returned to the task at hand not realizing I'd seen one of my father's ghosts until much, much later.

My father had been the last man alive who'd participated in the events that day, the only one who apparently ever spoke of it, and he'd passed the memory to me.

"I was sitting here," he said after we trudged to the top of the rise the summer before I turned thirty nine. He showed me where each of the men had been standing or sitting that day. "Your granddad was back here, behind me to the right. Over there, Smitty, and next to him was Mr. Johnson and Woody stood next to the wash tub of beer. Sammy Ledbetter stood here, to my left, and on the other side of him were Postmaster Wilson and Harley Pitzer, eight years before we sent him to Congress."

My father pointed to the horizon. "The train stopped two miles west of here. It must have been about one o'clock because we'd had lunch at the house before driving out. They opened up a couple of the box cars and herded them people into the scrub toward us."

My father turned his back on the memory and stood facing me. He had crumpled in on himself over the years and he leaned heavily on an aluminum walker. His skin had grown as dark and leathery as his eye patch and thin wisps of white hair lay across the top of his nearly-bald pate.

"Afterward, Harley and Smitty walked into the scrub and kicked over the bodies. I heard three more shots before your granddad bundled me into the Ford and carried me to the doctor. Hunting accident, he told the doctor and that's all that was ever said about it."

I took another swallow of beer and squinted against the midday sun, wishing I'd remembered my sunglasses.

A week before his death, my father called out my name from his hospital bed. He'd been blind for nearly a year by then and he couldn't see that I sat only a few feet away. I rose from the chair and took his hand.

"They're coming for me," he whispered hoarsely. "I can see them coming over the horizon, rising from the heat. They've taken all the others."

He coughed, and his entire body shook. Then he called out for granddad and for the next three days nothing he said made sense to anyone but me. The killing fields had never been discovered, the dead never reported as missing, and not one of the participants had ever revealed the things they had done.

Yet, the sins of my father became mine. I remembered details of what he had told me so well that I could see the entire day unfold around me. I took one last swallow of warm beer from the open bottle between my legs, wiped the palms of my hands on the thighs of my Levi's, then slid my father's deer rifle from its padded case.

I raised the rifle to my shoulder and took careful aim at the dead Mexicans swarming the horizon.

Carla Hartsfield   *Waxahachie*

BRAHMS & ANGELO'S GARAGE

It might be the perfect way to listen to a concerto.
The parking lot of an east-end McDonald's.
CBC radio and the New York Philharmonic.
A sausage McMuffin, hold the egg.
New Technology plugged
into The Age Of Enlightenment.
1962 and Lenny Bernstein.
Glenn Gould conducting his
special-order intellect from a corner in Fran's,
where he ate a plate of eggs
every morning over the papers.
And managed headlines in the key of D minor
with his week-long rehearsal
of a quirky standard.
Then there's me and Angelo
next to an American standard—
stick shift, that is. He's
using his wrench like a maestro—

car parts vibrate; at least,
I hear low-level humming going on.
But that might be Gould making counterpoint
where only he can hear it—
though *it's right, it's incredible*;
whenever I play Brahms I need larger arms,
kind of like Angelo here. I need a brawny body,
a Five O' Clock shadow, and unmuffled tone
that motors to the back row of Carnegie Hall.
I'm already halfway through my Sausage McMuffin,
and Gould is still making his way through
the second harmonic transition
in the extended, contrapuntal recapitulation;
I see the whole orchestra as a toolbox
with bolts (wind section),

nuts (strings, *especially violas*),
drills (trumpets and horns),
tubes hanging down from hydraulic lifts
(percussion and harp). Nobody believed,
especially Bernstein, that Brahms

was supposed to sound like this,
except maybe Gould and Brahms and me
trying hard not to get monkey grease
or cheese grease onto any part of our
not-yet-dead musical anatomies. Nobody expected,
especially Bernstein, that they might be wrong—
that Gould in his youth had the idea of the century.
To project Brahms like fine, curved chrome.
To shine it up into a vintage car.
To get the dumbbell piston
to meet the pianist halfway.
When the fine-tuning is done,
what you're left with is Glenn,
brilliant and shy in a leatherette booth
enjoying his breakfast, the sheen
still crystal on his genius;
and *the eggs, the eggs,*
because a Toronto cook
cranked them out so fast.
Are you listening, Lenny,
now that the mechanics and critics
have assembled into one symphonic entity
in Angelo's garage?
Hear Gould emanating boldly
with original lightness
into that recycled cup
that got stuck in the pipe.

Alicia Zavala Galván   *San Antonio*

PEQUEÑA

Dejame hacerme pequeña,
para que me guardes
en la palma de tu mano,
en la calidez de tus aceites,
reposar en tus lineas de vida,
rozando tus montes,
donde dejare
veredas nuevas de memoria.

¡Sí!-Dejame hacerme pequeña
como un grano de arena,
caminando contigo de aquí para alla
y de alla para acá.

y si la vida quiere,
con tú amor
volverme en perla

SMALL

Let me become small
so that you can hold me
in the palm of your hand,
in the warm of your oils,
repose in the lines of your life,
brushing against your mountains,
where I will leave
new paths of memory

Yes!-Let me become small
like a grain of sand,
traveling with you from here to there
and from there to here.

and if life wants,
with your love
become a pearl

Linda S. Bingham   *Wimberley*

MARILU'S BAPTISM

It was the second time in a month I had seen Marilu Herring in church. The first time was the funeral service for her husband Edwin who died at the age of sixty-eight after a long illness. The second, and much more surprising occasion, was Marilu's baptism. Surprising, in that neither of us belonged to that church–or any other for that matter.

Langston and I knew Marilu and Edwin Herring socially, not intimately. Both our houses backed up to the 7th fairway. Often Marilu and I met across a bridge table. Nothing I knew of her up to that point led me to expect she was a religious person.

Yet, I was the one she asked to witness her receiving a few drops of sanctified water on her stiff coiffure. The church was of no particular denomination, or rather it was one of those all-inclusive Protestant "interdenominational" fellowships. Not being a regular member there, I couldn't judge if the congregants were surprised to see a gray-haired woman being baptized. The minister conducted the slight affair with becoming solemnity, and moments later Marilu was back in her place beside me in the pew. Out of the corner of my eye I saw her dab her nose with a tissue. I wondered what it all meant to her.

She accepted my invitation to lunch, perhaps feeling, as I did, that something more was called for. Over salads at a Sunday-crowded restaurant, I put the question to her.

"Marilu, why did you do this?"

The quickness of her response told me she had anticipated my question. "There was no one to stop me."

I can only report that her face bore traces of what might be called "radiance."

"I had no idea you harbored, well, convictions," I said. "You mean that you wanted to go to church, wanted to, er, get baptized, but Edwin wouldn't let you?"

"Not exactly. He was raised in the church and was baptized himself years ago. It was just that we lived a certain kind of lifestyle, as you know. Now no one expects anything of me."

"I'm not very religious myself, Marilu. You might've asked someone better qualified, someone who understands it better. I confess that the symbolism of dumping a handful of tepid water over your nice new hairdo quite escapes me. Do you plan to go to church regularly now?"

Serene, Marilu smiled. "I'm not sure yet. I think I'll wait and see how I feel."

It occurred to me that the poor woman had fallen under the influence of the minister, a Mr. Lackey, who had both buried her husband and done the sprinkling. Langston and I had met him at the hospital when Edwin lay dying. Perhaps Marilu's terror in that awful hour was the impetus for calling in a clergyman? To what effect, I wondered? Had Edwin confessed his sins–or whatever they call it these days–there at the last when he surely knew that time was running out? Would I myself undergo a similar change of heart when push came to shove?

It is unsettling to think that one is subject to a complete reversal in one's thinking in the face of inevitable biological function, i.e., death. My own feelings about God are that He surely exists, if one need put a name to the natural order of things, to Nature herself, the cosmos, mathematics, music, art. But it is absurd to think that such a Being needs our obeisance and prayers, our hymns and candles, requires us to dress up on Sunday mornings and sit on a hard pew. Pardon if I misquote Emily Dickinson, but I quite agree with her that Sunday mornings are too nice to spend in church. For myself, a golf course will do.

I started to say some of this to Marilu but I didn't want to ruin her moment. Actually, I don't mind at all if other people go to church. Don't mind if they talk in tongues and indulge in all that other mumbo-jumbo either, so long as they leave me to my pagan delights. So, I tried to support whatever quest Marilu was on. I spent the rest of my time with Marilu catching her up on news of mutual acquaintances she had missed during Edwin's illness. Afterward, we went our separate ways.

The following month I was busy organizing the Ladies Golf Association Charity Tournament, which benefited our local food bank. I thought of offering Marilu one of the committees, but found myself facing a familiar dilemma: Do the recently bereaved wish to be included or to be left alone? I had known several widows and found this to be an individual matter. In the end, I did nothing and it was quite some time before I saw my friend again. Guiltily, I realized that I hadn't seen her at the bridge table lately. Was she isolating herself? But no, she seemed to be with a friend now.

"Marilu, you look wonderful!" I told her.

Indeed, she looked ten years younger, her hair colored a soft brown that I suspect was its original color.

"This is Betsy Williams," she said, introducing me to her friend.

In the exchange of pleasantries that followed, I discovered no intersection of my life with Betsy's. Twice Marilu mentioned some activity that had taken place at church, from which I deduced she had become a regular member.

I'm sorry to say that even more time elapsed before I saw Marilu again. Her husband's death had divided us, our two lives falling to either side like waves against a prow. I, not being the one whose circumstances changed, continued on the same course, but I could only suppose that Marilu had found different activities and friends. She didn't sign up to play club tournaments that year.

I noticed the Herring house go on the market. Every time I passed, the For Sale sign reminded me of the odd scene Marilu had asked me to witness: A middle-aged woman standing for baptism. The robed and solemn minister reciting a ritualistic prayer as he swept open a small domed chalice and reached in for a surprisingly generous handful of water. She, somewhat taller in her high-heeled shoes, stooped to accommodate his reach. The water ran away on all sides, some of it dribbling down Marilu's forehead and channeling alongside her nose. Maybe that was what I had seen her wiping away, holy water, not tears.

In my years jiggering with actuarial figures for the insurance board, I learned that white females in this country may expect to live 79.2 years, while their male counterparts can only achieve 72.7. It is not surprising then that hardly two years after Marilu Herring lost her husband, I lost mine. I had plenty of time for quiet reflection those last days of his life, regrettably spent on the fourth floor of M.D. Anderson Hospital.

Often my thoughts turned to Marilu Herring and how her life had changed after losing her husband. Was I hiding from myself a desire to call a minister to help me through this experience? In any case, it wasn't necessary. Our society has come up with an alternative to churchy funeral rites: a secular service held in a funeral home. I find them rather bland myself, like a pot of beans you've forgotten to salt. But Langston was far too ill to consult in the matter, and in the end I was left–as so many women are, as Marilu had been–to arrange things as I thought best.

I decided to make Langston's burial a quiet celebration of earthly Elysium. A string quartet played a Bach air. The casket was decorated with rough bouquets of wildflowers. Our daughter Caroline read a poem that her father had liked, the one about laughing Allegra and Edith with the golden hair.

I cannot report that as a result of my husband's death I was moved to go to church, or that I discovered a need to have holy water sprinkled on my brow. But I did find that life simply did not go on as before. I felt subtly excluded from the social life I had enjoyed, even denied the opportunity to talk about Langston among well-meaning friends. I recalled doing the same thing to Marilu, changing the subject rather than let the subject linger on things she would rather forget.

I marked the first anniversary of Langston's passing by ordering a pair of tickets to the symphony, force of habit prompting me to ask for two. As I mentally ticked off an increasingly meager list of friends I might ask to go with me, I realized that most of our friends had been couples. I thought of Marilu. Is this what it comes to? I wondered. Are my only companions to be other widows? When I reached Marilu, the first thing I did was apologize for my amazing lack of sensitivity, although I still didn't know what to make of that business of getting baptized.

Marilu brushed off my apology. "Don't give it another thought. You can't be expected to read another person's thoughts. I'd be happy to go to the symphony with you. I was so sorry, Janice, to hear of your loss. I would have come to the funeral if I hadn't been in Europe at the time."

"I understand better about your loss now that I've gone through it myself. Tell me, Marilu, if you don't mind my asking. When you got baptized, did you feel–well, I don't quite know how to phrase this–did you feel that it would lead to your being reunited with Edwin in the great by-and-by? You said that he had been baptized."

"No, I don't think that was it, exactly. I just felt a need to purge the cold horrible presence of death. A clean start. You know, like in your work, totting up the balance or whatever. Then you start fresh."

"And it helped to have the minister pray over you and sprinkle the holy water?"

"We all face the terrors in our own way. It seems that yours is to buy symphony tickets."

I attempted a laugh. "I've always been uncomfortable with the religious stuff. Having worked with numbers all my life, I feel that their precision and predictability are better evidence of divine order than any mystical twaddle you might hear from the pulpit."

"Oh, Janice! I've always thought you so brave and sensible! The thought of you was a marvelous consolation that first awful year after Edwin's death."

"Me? Why, you surprise me very much! I suppose...well, I suppose the thought of you has given _me_ some comfort, Marilu, the thought of that holy water running down your face...."

"See you Sunday," she said.

"Sunday?"

"For the symphony."

"Oh, yes, the symphony. They're playing Haydn and Bach."

"Thank you for thinking of me."

"Thank you for making room for me in your busy schedule."

Marilu laughed merrily, a sound I envied. Would I ever really laugh again? "Oh, yes! In my busy busy schedule."

Walt McDonald   *Lubbock*

AFTER THE FUNERAL

The tide grinds stones to meal,
sea pudding with a crust, mincemeat
of scallions, plankton,

stringy bits of crabs. Gulls
glide and dive, or hunker down
and bob between waves,

scooping whatever's there,
like children dipping fingers in
and licking tips of chocolate

and knuckles of meringue.
We tip shells over with toes of boots,
scoop them with thick gloved hands

like paws. Bundled, we turn
into the wind and blink, gusts
on the coast at Kitty Hawk

past forty, wind chill below freezing,
the spray like bits of ice.
Only the desperate are here

the day after Christmas, like us,
two thousand miles from home,
too far to drive back, not yet.

Walt McDonald   *Lubbock*

SOMEONE PEDDLING HOME

Lately at night a light goes by—
that pump, that waver and bob's
a bicycle light, someone peddling home

or off to the pond to gig frogs.   ·
No bother, the trail so far away
gears grind without sound, a clank

sometimes when a tire drops down
in a chug hole. This far in the country,
coyotes watch. I wait on the porch

and rock, sipping coffee. Almost time
for my turn at the hospital,
grandmother after surgery.

The light's a constant firefly
without an off switch, dim glow
with no beam showing on the road.

Through the trees, it flicks
and flitters, blinks out
behind the hedge, pops on

and off again, gone south
without a tail light
and the coyotes howl.

James Hoggard   *Witchita Falls*

REDTAIL HAWK

Its feathers roughed by the north wind,
the hawk stayed fast on its live oak perch,
then slowly, as if releasing its breath in its wings,
it rose, higher now, then planed away fast
from the leafless mott, and it wouldn't return
till talons and beak had been washed
    in a hot splash-bath of blood

SPRING STORMS

We were well into spring,
the crocuses long gone,
the long high heat back,
low smoky clouds turning,

and irises blooming,
then a late April norther
iced the turbulent air
The sky then went still,

threateningly still,
till gusting winds,
stirring dust and molds,
reddened the heavens

Andrew Geyer   *Lubbock*

WHITE SANDS

White. White is a world without an ocean.

White is sand as far as the eye can see.

These white gypsum dunes would be the most sensuous beach in the world if they only had an ocean to slither blue fingers across them. The dunes remember the sinuous touch of high tide. In search of a body of azure curves, driven by a southwest wind that smells of desert mountains, the white waves of sand advance—growing, cresting, slumping forward to embrace a shallow inland sea that is no longer there.

White evaporates. Vanishes into thin air.

Gypsum comes from the Greek language, meaning "to cook the earth." The dunes, some as high as sixty feet, consist of gypsum crystals deposited in an ancient ocean bed. Gypsum, a hydrous form of calcium sulfate—$CaSO_4.2H_2O$— is rarely found in the form of sand, because it is soluble in water. Rain and snow fall in the surrounding mountains, dissolve gypsum from the rocks, carry it down into the Tularosa Basin. Normally, the dissolved gypsum would then be carried by rivers to the sea. But no river drains the Tularosa Basin. The water, along with the gypsum it contains, is trapped. As the water evaporates, the dissolved gypsum is deposited onto the desert floor.

Red. Red is Jacob's jacket.

Red is a three year-old blur rolling over and over down the slip-face of a sixty-foot dune. Red is a three year-old boy's cries of joy.

The red sun would rather be sinking into the sea than into the dry San Andres Mountains. Red is the color of my wife's hair. Unlike the dunes, which are blinding white as the surface of the moon, Elizabeth does not seek the embrace of an ocean. She sits in the shadow of a dune holding her knees, watching me slog up the slip-face with Jacob choo-chooing on my shoulders. His red jacket flaps in the wind, the sand stings our eyes as we make the top of the slope in one headlong scrambling rush. We sit side-by-side on the crest of the wave. Jacob is grinning at me, a grin as wide and white as a field of dunes.

Blue. Blue is the color of Jacob's eyes.

Blue is an absent ocean. Blue is a desert sky over soft white waves of sand. Blue is a moment that cannot be recaptured as my son rolls over and over back down the steep slip-face of the dune.

White is gypsum. Gypsum is very soft—a "2" on the ten-point hardness scale where "1" equals talc and "10" equals diamond. The white sand glistens like diamonds when it catches the sun. My wife's fingernails, painted red, are a "2 .5" on the hardness scale. My wife's red nails, which also glisten, could scratch the gypsum crystals like soft white skin.

White is a function of wind. Strong southwest winds blow across the playa, pick up gypsum particles, carry them downwind. As the sand grains accumulate into dunes, they bounce up the windward slope, creating ripples on the surface. At the steep leading edge of the dune, sand builds up until gravity pulls it down the slip-face, moving the dune forward.

White is suspension, saltation, surface creep. White is the movement of sand. The wind whipping the gypsum into the air bleaches the horizon, fading the mountains gray-white and making it seem as though the dunes are on the verge of achieving flight. The Great Lakes lie 1,400 miles northeast, directly downwind. I have never seen a Great Lake. But in pictures they all look very blue. I wonder if the dunes, which have not felt the touch of a liquid body in more than 250 million years, would settle for freshwater and an absence of surf.

Red is a three-year old boy's cries of joy. Deep blue is the coming evening. White is the dunes seeking to stretch themselves out on thin air.

The Gulf of Mexico, out of which the red sun rose this morning, is deep blue and salty. But it lies eight hundred miles away in a direction the wind never blows. It lies in the direction the three of us came from, the direction in which we will return home. But home lies far short of the ocean. Like the dunes, which are turning red now in the light of the setting sun, I have not touched a body of water in too long a while. The only time I have ever seen Elizabeth swim in the ocean was on our honeymoon, and I am convinced Jacob was conceived that evening, on soft white sand, just beyond the dark fingers of incoming tide.

Timothy R. Morris   *Arlington*

DOWN ON I-30

Over my maple logs one morning, I run out of comics and turn aimlessly through the paper. I stop at the death notices. Nothing out of the ordinary. Mother of three, age 48. Homemaker, age 94. Retired from the aerospace industry, age 67. After a long battle with cancer, age 51.

I realize all at once that I am going to die. Not during this maple log, but eventually. At 48, or 51, or 67, or 94. For most of my life, if there's been any way of avoiding something, I've avoided it. Swimming lessons, college commencement, registering for the draft, voting in pointless primaries, applying for good jobs in places I didn't want to move to, learning to ride a bike, watching the last game of playoff series my team was obviously going to lose, growing up, asking Beth Perlmutter to the senior prom, scanning downloaded files for viruses, orthodontia, sharpening my lawn mower blades at regular intervals —you name it, I've skipped it.

And here's something—that obituary page impresses upon me relentlessly—that I will just not be able to skip. No teacher is going to appear and exempt me from that final exam. No benefactor is going to show up and write me a check so I don't have to take that lousy part-time job. Nobody's going to offer me a ride so I don't have to take that Greyhound from Pittsburgh to Cleveland. I am going to die. And unlike the nuclear collapse of the sun or the final degradation of all chemical atoms into iron, my death is going to occur in my own lifetime, or rather, to be exact, just the tiniest of bits afterwards.

This insight rates a fourth maple log, which leaves me thirsty and even more dispirited. I leave a note on my door canceling my 10 and 11 o'clocks and get in the car. I drive up one street for a couple of miles and back down a parallel street. I'm going to die, there will be nothing left of me. One moment I am conscious of everything, of a drawing Gemma's done for her art class, of a sharp cold wind that's blowing across Texas, of remembering Mary Ann's mouth, and the next thing, all these awarenesses will evaporate.

I drive on, numb. I get to Eastbourne Marketplace, on I-30 in farthest east Fort Worth. This sounds like a fascinating bazaar full of haggling merchants, but it's actually just a big strip mall with a Toys R Us and a Target. I go into the Target and walk the candy aisles, very slowly. Up and down, back and forth, past wax cola bottles, bullseyes, string licorice, Jolly Ranchers, oh dear God Jolly Ranchers, circus peanuts, Jujyfruits, Mike and that sinister little bastard Ike.

I have to have something, some candy, some sweet thing that has only good memories attached, something that will take care of me and will not cloy. But with a bag of toffee in one hand and a box of Milk Duds in the other, I am torn and tortured. I can't buy candy. I let them drop back into the rack.

I go over to the books. Finding Your Precocious Self. Letting Loved Ones Go, why would anyone want to do that. Men are from some planet, women are from some other planet, everybody's an alien, nobody's from earth. Oprah Book Club, read about how people win through anguish and despair to a fuller life. Can't I take a short-cut? Am I really the better for this anguish?

I wander out. There's a Santa in shirtsleeves, ringing a bell above a red metal pot. I go into the craft store next door. There are probably better places to cope with a blinding fear of death than a suburban strip-mall craft store. I walk every aisle, looking for some answers. One aisle is full of blank paper bags. There are ten thousand thousand of them, pastel, brown, black, red and green for Christmas. There's an aisle of unfinished wooden boxes, waiting to be personalized. Their hardware is flimsy and glued-on. Ready for that special someone's name, for that back of that special someone's closet, for that special someone's attic, for that special someone's yard sale. Ready to burn in that special someone's house fire, to be tossed in the garbage by that special someone's grandchildren, to be stripped to its atoms again and to plunge with the rest of the universe into heat death, to ride between stars for all eternity as a cinder, World's Best Dad.

In one aisle of the store, a woman is conducting a scrapbooking class. Her hair and lips are the same color as Mary Ann's, but she's a good deal older. She smiles persistently. She's telling the class some ideas for themed pages.

"Here," she says, holding up a sample scrapbook, "I have arranged all things that have to do with memories of my son's senior year as letterman on the football team. You can do this sort of thing with your own memories. And then with the memories left over" —she holds up a plank of wood with a heavy coat of varnish— "you can decoupage keepsake items. They make handy gifts, the gift of memory."

I sit on a stray chair in the next aisle over. I want to teach a class in forget-booking. "Take these cocktail napkins from Troppo Gelato, class. See this one with her pink lipstick on it? I'm going to take this one" —fold, fold— "and drop it in this beaker of vodka. When I apply the match" —swoosh— "it goes up in a lovely flambé. Pretty soon you'll have forgotten the restaurant and the date and even the shade of the lipstick.

"Now, for those stubborn memories, paste your snapshots on a pistol target and take it to the range. A few clips of 9mm ammunition will blast these annoying pictures away." This isn't funny. I get up and wander over to a display case full of miniature china animals. A dozen perky puppies look out at me: splayed bassets, poodles sitting at attention, stolid St. Bernards, playful Dalmatians, a cocker all fur. All staring sightlessly at me. When it's dark in the store, after hours, they stare out at nothing at all. When I am dead, I will stare at nothing. I will have no more trouble with memory.

I walk down an aisle of Christmas Picks. Dozens of bushel baskets brim with plastic holly, plastic presents, plastic Santas, plastic sugarplums, plastic candy canes, each one mounted on a little plastic spear. The spear is evidently the "Pick" part; it's decoration by impalement. Plastic stretches out festively around me for the better part of an acre, plastic things made by starving children in China, accumulated here at this arid, barren end of the earth where nobody wants them. $2.79 marked down (twice) to $1.49, no takers.

Beyond the Pick Parade there's one last aisle, an aisle of model kits. I used to make models when I was a kid. I never painted them. My models were an albino world of white polystyrene where everything—ships, planes, cars, space-craft, the Incredible Hulk—was a washed-out off-white. They're in my mom's attic in Syosset now, cycling through the Northeastern seasons, melting a bit each August, freezing back again in December, losing their form, sliding down toward decay. Maybe I'll buy a model. Maybe making things will restore me to good spirits. I look for a 1999 Suburban that I can paint forest green. They don't sell models of Suburbans. It isn't the pre-teen fantasy car, I guess. It's the fantasy car of smitten grey-haired 40ish therapists. "As we finished our chicken-fried-steak sandwiches at Thatsaburger, she drained her chocolate shake and looked lasciviously at me. I swept her up and carried her off in my Suburban."

Nancy Fitz-Gerald Viens   *Denton*

GALVESTON CATS

Galveston cats come out at night
Like derelicts along the seawall,
Hunting scraps of fishheads
Tossed underneath the pier,
Eyeballs staring like burnished steel,
A tasty treat to dampen down the belly's
Crawling hunger for a meal.
Tigers, greys and calicos
Rumble along, tails tall and high
Switching in feral umbrage there,
Warning dogs and fishermen
Not to venture too near—
BEWARE!

They search for rats that scuttle through
The rocks and drainage pipes,
Big Macs abandoned near the wooden stair
On which the gaudy tourists trudge
Down to the tar-speckled beach.
They raid the garbage cans
Sticky with Coke and week-old beer,
Cornucopias of discarded sandwiches,
Pizza crusts and rancid cheese.
They raucously mate wherever they please
And all the good folk can hear.

Galveston cats thrive and prosper,
While the weak are winnowed out
By traffic and disease.
Their progeny are lean and mean—
They gaze about with wary eye
From grim stone parapets
On all intruders to their hard-won turf,
And stalk the saucy little sea birds
Prancing in the salty surf.

Charles P. Stites   *Austin*

FOREBEARANCE

You cannot say "Texan" in a whisper,
I have found.
The name demands a resonance,
An expansion of the chest,
And a pause in its wake
For the inevitable awe to be registered.

Somewhere back in my blood
Was a dusty explorer
Who, mapless and reckless,
Managed to weather the weather,
And outlast Commanche and Confederacy.

Then, up came the courthouses, schools,
And the dry goods stores.
Those pioneers left these
Skeletons of empire,
Wild-flavored legends,
And, eventually, me.

I have seen the old ones,
Who are leaving us,
One by one,
And they seem to be
Of a close, yet separate, race.
Their leathered skins,
Their unleavened accents,
And their curious manners,
Conspire to make them appear foreign.
Their fathers and mothers
Bested the frontier,
While they themselves
Wrested it back from droughts and dust.

It is an oddity
That they should leave an heir like me
With a legacy of easy life.
I am grateful,
Yet theirs is a gift that also steals.

My great, great-grand ones
Crouched sweatily in cabins,
Ready to fight for what they had taken,
And in an unbroken, or seeming, line,
That ferocity has been passed to me.

I hold on to that birthright,
Thinking on it,
As I look on the gallon of cold milk in my hand,
Two days past expiration,
Pondering its safety,

And whether I should drink.

DANCING WITH FRED AND FREUD

A lifelong puzzle for me is how Fred Astaire could stick his hands into his pants pockets and stroll up a flight of steps looking even more debonair than usual, while I—when I jam my hands into my pockets and mount a flight of steps, I always look as though I am on the way to the unemployment relief agency.

Maybe part of it was Fred's clear-eyed, All American conduct. While there was magic in the way he danced Ginger Rogers around those art deco film sets in the 'thirties, he discreetly never kissed her on camera. Unlike Cary Grant and Clark Gable, who had sexual smoke running out their ears all during the same era. Fred was above all that, true blue, classy, hewing to The Code.

Yet what are the mechanics involved in Fred's tap dancing and stair climbing? How much is what he does, and how much is what Astaire simply is? In the last line of "Among School Children," Yeats asks how anyone can separate a dancer from his dance. Finding the answer has been my lifelong quest.

During the year in which Astaire was "Puttin' on the Ritz" in *Blue Skies*, I was among school children myself, a high school sophomore in a little West Texas town, and I got my first lesson in dancing on the floor of our living room one winter afternoon. The big war was won, the troops were home, and dancing was becoming an important social event in our little town. A shy lad, I had nevertheless noticed the two step was an acceptable way to get close to girls.

I was sitting around that afternoon with two of my grungy pals, listening to Glenn Miller's "String of Pearls" whirl off at seventy-eight revolutions per minute, when I let it drop that I had never learned to dance. They first expressed disbelief in the manner of teenagers who discover a friend is ignorant of something they themselves mastered only a week or so before. Then my guests offered to teach me—for twenty-five cents.

A quarter wasn't much even then, so I bought. Solo demonstration first. Next I partnered with one pal, maneuvering like a man with plaster casts on both legs. It would have been more fun with a girl. With say, the beautiful, blonde Penny Price, whom I had admired from afar. But more embarrassing also. For a teen, embarrassment is feared more than cancer. A week later my mother showed me how to waltz, and I was ready to try real girls. But I was a long way from Fred Astaire.

***

My classmate and best friend, Rudy Hopson, commented: "At the end of every war, there is a great moral letdown. And we are living right in the middle of it. Whoopee!"

In those adolescent days, however, the blisses of physical sex, like Plato's ideal forms, existed as abstractly for me as they had for Fred and Ginger in the 'thirties. I began spasmodically dating girls—although not the gorgeous, yellow-haired Penny Price. I asked out girls with roughly the same amount of dating experience as I had.

Arrangements for each date confronted me with complex questions. Which girl should I ask? Could I get the family car? Should I blurt out an invitation in the school hallway, or to better shield my timidity, hope to find an uninhabited moment in our family kitchen where our telephone was rooted?

Making witty small talk during an evening out was the next big challenge. (If I had stood back from my own embarrassment even slightly, I would have seen that any shy girl foolish enough to accept my advances was not listening to me anyway, but was desperately searching for something witty to say herself.) All this unimaginably difficult foreplay led up to a chaste goodnight kiss before she vanished behind her parents' door.

***

During the year Astaire teamed with Gene Kelly to tap and sing "The Babbitt and the Bromide" in *Ziegfeld Follies*, I happened one day to be hanging around a local gift shop, which carried a few books. Thumbing through a Modern Library edition of *Great Expectations*, I heard the sales clerk and Lottie Hopson discussing a rash of promiscuity among young marrieds. Lottie, a funny shaped girl, top heavy with skinny hips, was rumored to have slept around widely before her marriage to the older brother of my best friend. I assumed Lottie brought real insight into these matters.

"Read Sigmund Freud," Lottie advised the clerk. "He explains these things. You need to stock his books here."

Aha! Soon after, my family visited Mom's relatives in Dallas, and I went to the Baptist Bookstore to purchase *A General Introduction to Psychoanalysis*. And by george, Freud did explain everything.

Freud never made a more fanatic convert. When a buddy told me about a dream in which he fox trotted with a local rancher's daughter, I explained that dreams were wish fulfillments and that dancing was a symbol of sexual intercourse. My pal quit telling me his dreams.

It wasn't until I matured a few more years that I realized everything is a sex symbol with Freud. Yet with all its high minded appeal to our aesthetic sense, dancing truly has a low, underground link with Shakespeare's "beast with two backs." Maybe this too is connected with Yeats' query about distinguishing dancer from dance.

***

Fundamentalist preachers—there was no other kind in our little town—condemned dancing, a hangover from the era when hard drinking cowboys rode into town once a month to whoop it up with gaudy girls they found in rowdy dance halls. This led to a local, somewhat unbiblical, eleventh commandment: "Thou shalt not two-step." It added a delicious taint of minor sin to our primitive shuffles, but deprived us of most public places in which to stomp.

Teenage stratagems arose. For instance, after the hand hold games, and the cake, and the gift-wrap ripping, at a cheerleader's birthday party in October, we sardined into four autos—I rode in a dinky Ford coupe with a chubby girl crushing my lap—and scorched off to Seven Mile Park, a little roadside picnic area built for travelers by the WPA.

Two eighteen-wheelers had moored in the park ahead of us, drivers obviously snoozing, so we pushed on two miles farther and extemporized by stationing our paired vehicles on opposites of the highway, facing each other with headlights shining. Hardly an art deco dance floor. Windows were cranked down and all available car radios (two) were tuned and twisted full blast to a station playing "Nice Work If You Can Get It."

On the next number, Rodgers and Hart's "Lover," I paired with the chubby girl to waltz across the highway. Suddenly a cattle truck topped the hill at seventy miles an hour, scattering us like billiard balls. Miraculously, nobody was squashed. But it was "Goodnight Sweetheart" for our party.

By fits and starts I got better at both dancing and dating. During my senior year, the year Astaire whirled Judy Garland around in *Easter Parade*, our little town relaxed its taboo on dancing. Why? Returning World War II veterans now filled every spare room in town, and many of them had acquired a pagan taste for two-stepping across USO floors. The guardians of our morals looked the other way to accommodate returning Ulysses. We high school students openly scheduled dances in the big fire department meeting room on the second floor of the city hall.

***

Most exciting by far were the street dances on weekends that the veterans themselves staged. Fiddlers and guitar players—the county had a surprisingly large pool of them—climbed up on a cotton trailer and filled the courthouse square with "You Are My Sunshine" and "Born to Lose." You could scrape off a pair of new leather soles during a single evening on those paved streets.

Meanwhile, I had finally worked up enough nerve to ask pretty blonde Penny Price to a couple of movies, and surprise, she accepted. So I asked her to a street dance.

Penny Price—yes, there were a good many jokes about her name—was a great stepper. A class ahead of me, she had already graduated and was working as a clerk in a big clothing store downtown. Homer Hopson, older brother of my best friend, Rudy, also worked in the store with Penny. Homer was a veteran, hero of the PX at Fort Bliss, husband of Freudian Lottie. When Penny and I had been at the dance a few minutes, Homer spotted us and traipsed over to ask Penny for a waltz. I surrendered her and took a turn or two around the street with someone else.

After a bit, Homer's Lottie came around. Lottie, beauty of the big bosom and skinny behind. She asked:

"Have you seen Homer?"

"He was out shaking a leg with Penny."

"But where are they now?"

We began snooping among the cars parked along the outskirts, among the clusters of revelers talking or flirting or taking a snort of booze, in doorways, in alleys, on the courthouse lawn. Lottie got more and more disturbed as it became increasingly clear that Penny and Homer were no longer available.

At Lottie's suggestion, we hopped in my car and drove to the Hopson residence. We rushed through, flipping on lights in the living room, the kitchen, the nursery—the Hopson children had been farmed out to their grandmother for the evening—and finally into the master bedroom. Nobody.

Lottie plopped down on the bed.

"That dirty rat!" The word, "rat," was strong condemnation in Lottie's genteel vocabulary.

"Maybe things aren't as bad as they look," I said.

"I'll pay him back for this!"

Lottie bounced a little on the bed as she uttered her threat. When she looked up at me, the air in the bedroom was suddenly humid with sex.

I became intensely aware that Lottie, who had led me to Freud, was a pretty young woman of no more than twenty-six years, full breasted, and in spite of her odd shape, desirable.

She was also, however, a mother, married, and married to the older brother of my best friend, Rudy. Totally off limits by Fred's code.

"I bet they are back at the party," I said.

"Wait a minute. Let me think." Lottie crossed her legs casually, which caused her skirt to retreat above her knees. She took out a cigarette and lit it. She offered me one.

I had experimented with cigarettes, but I declined to go close enough to take that coffin nail from her. I felt as bumbling as Fred Astaire in one of his comedy sequences.

"They're probably at the dance someplace," I said.

Lottie sighed, smiled, and rose. We walked back through the house, turning out lights as we went. I'm fairly sure I didn't look as jaunty as Fred exiting with Ginger. Lottie and I climbed in my car in silence, drove back to the street dance.

A half hour later Penny and Homer turned up with a lame story about taking a sick guitar strummer home.

The rest of the evening for Penny and me was—what can I call it?—uneasy, cool, distanced. I took her home early.

Well, I've never really regretted refusing to help Lottie avenge herself. If I can't strut like Fred Astaire, I can at least act as honorably as he always did in those 'thirties and 'forties musicals. Yet occasionally, I wonder what that odd-shaped gal would have looked like with her clothing removed.

Robin Reid   *Commerce*

JANUARY 29, 2000

The January storm left coats
on every blade and branch, ice
an inch thick. Shining
spears catch the light,
throw it back in shouts of silver
and destroy any thought of cold.

I never thought of Texas as cold
and when I moved left winter coats
in my mother's closet. Silver
shards fringe the roof and ice
carpets the yard, the light
through clouds of passing gray shining

bright enough to blind. The shining
air cuts into lungs, cold
shuddering through blood; light
moves inside organs and coats
all warmth and movement in ice.
My breath puffs out, silver

into the winter air. Miles of silver
fields and trees surround me, shining
in the falling light, turned from hard ice
to fantasy spun from water and cold.
The trees wear coats
of mail, bear weapons made of light.

I remember the summer heat, light
pounding down from a silver
sky. Mornings, light coats
of dew left green leaves shining
and cardinals singing. The cold
breath of tea poured over ice

cooled parched throats. Now ice
replaces green and red, all light
sharpened by the winter cold
turning the world to silver.
Without heat, the sun, shining,
cannot penetrate the coats

of clear ice. The blinding silver
moves light as cats, shining
eyes shut against cold, warm in plush coats.

J. Paul Holcomb   *Double Oak*

O BROTHER WHERE ART THOU, 1959

The members weren't hazing us.

They were helping us pledges bond.
Never mind it was midnight Friday
and we had been taken south of town
with sacks over our heads
and offered community by a creek.
The members rushed back to town,
happy hyenas trailing hysterical laughter
heavy on the road back to campus.

Remarkably we did bond, all but one.
Like the lone defector at the Alamo,
he crossed the creek-line and raced
fast like a half Cherokee can
to the nearest phone and called
for help from his brother in town.

Meanwhile we yelled beside the creek,
tried to number ourselves, counting again
and again. Afraid we had failed at community,
we thought we were counting off wrong,
until one of us said that Wilson was gone.
We were indeed one short.

Another pledge saw the lights
of an approaching car, convinced us
that the Cherokee, bright as new light,
was coming back for his tribe, returning
for his family. Wilson arrived, and we
counted off once more, then crowded
into the car and followed the hyena trail,
making laugh-tracks of our own
in full-throated glee.

Marilyn Gilbert Komechak   *Fort Worth*

JUST ONE GOOD THING

Lizzie circles the yellow plastic kitchen table like a toy train on a wobbly track. Not once in her twenty years of marriage to Lester has she felt on solid ground. She places each chipped blue and white plate on a calico place mat. Lizzie's effort and the steam from the pot roast begin to fog her glasses. A few graying strands catch in the moisture of her cheek. *Lester's got to have his meat and potatoes.* She hears the hay balers' tramping feet echo on the back porch.

At the sink she looks out of the window into the barn lot with its great white barn. Its black letters leap out at her, LESTER JESSUP FARMS. This is the high point of the year for her husband, hay baling and selling off the calves. *He's gonna say what he's said for twenty years...take you for a little spin.*

She thinks about the annual trip to the K-mart and last year's plastic potted geraniums, fifty-five cents. On these trips Lester always cautions her to get...justonegood thing. Lizzie sighs.

Then about her gift from him: You know what with this year's crops, we're up-against-the-wall. Lizzie looks at the water-stained wall by the sink and feels the urge to hit her head on it. But, no, everybody likes Lester. *They'd think I had gone crazy.*

The red and white geraniums from last year face her on the windowsill. Lizzie grabs up the flowerpots and runs hot water over them. This only makes their dust ball-up in clumps. The red plastic has now faded to a ghastly pink. Putting them back on the shelf Lizzie feels queasy. *What's the matter with me?*

At that moment she hears her husband enter the kitchen. *He's in high spirits. He must have gotten a good price for the hay. I oughta be satisfied.*

The nausea is back and sweeps over her more strongly this time. She stands at the sink with her back to him. *Funny, that last wave almost felt cleansing.* Then in her mind's eye Lizzie sees the old tin canister in the back of the pantry. She waits until Lester is busy washing up. She fishes her hand back into its shadowy recesses. Her touch reassures her that it is still there. A little saved from the groceries for a year.

Maybe I should just go ahead and tell him I've been putting some back. But the thought frightens her. A sharp slap on the bottom. Lizzie, don't forget we're goin' for a little spin!

She tries to smile, but it is only a sideways lift of her mouth. Back at the sink, her fingers move lazily in the hot soapy suds over the gritty bottom of the iron skillet. *I ought to be thankful.* But her fingers keep moving over the rough surface, searching.

Lizzie, I'm talkin' to you. His voice lifting: we're gonna take that spin, so you get yourself ready. A wink this time.

Down the aisle she flies, past the stacks of towels, left at the T-shirts, then right at the bricabrac. She sees the purses piled on a table in front of her, *GENUINE LEATHER*. The soft brown leather melts under her touch. She can see Lester up at the front of the store, proud, puffed up, talking to the others. Takin' 'er for a birthday spin.

The brown leather feels good on her arm but the sickness washes over her again. *I'm just standin' here like a stump.* Lizzie looks over her shoulder. Her husband is still busy talking. She slips the money from her old plastic coin purse into a side pocket of the leather purse.

Now at the checkout counter: Jereen, do me a favor…money for the purse is in the side picket. Jereen nods. She smiles her eyes twinkling.

Lester comes to stand next to Lizzie at the cash register. He is looking a little worried. Jereen coos: Hi, Lester! Your wife's a good little shopper. Blue Light Special, $9.98. Lester's eyebrows arch. Little steep ain't it Jereen? He hesitates, then whacks the soft leather with his palm as he digs out his wallet with the other hand. Jereen and Lizzie give each other a look. They both know how extra generous he is with own his mother.

On the drive home, Lizzie clutches the purse with both hands as it lies in her lap. She feels a little lump. Jereen has returned Lester's money to a side pocket of the new purse. Smiling to herself, Lizzie thinks about next year, and how she'll get… justonegoodthing.

Mary Cimarolli   *Richardson*

DRAG RACING AT ENNIS

"Don't Red Light," I pray, knowing only
a few specific things to pray for.
I am your mother—but not part of your racing family.
I don't share your passion for cars and all things mechanical.
You don't have my ardor for poems and all things literary.
And yet, I can understand what we do share because
today I came to watch you race at Ennis.

Motors without mufflers roar for the race;
loudspeakers push into viewing stands.
Smells of spent fuel and burnt rubber;
smoke thick as fog;
front ends rise at green light's flash.
Sponsor's names, part of the car—like paint,
blur in the rush to be first.

Drag jockeys breathing life into cars—
spooked horses at the starting gate,
thoroughbreds ride, horse-like, to track in trailers.

Your car is tuned like a haiku;
engine honed to perfection,
body spotless, not a superfluous part—or comma.
You build your own motor in perfect sync,
revise endlessly, and when you don't win,
back for more revision—a good poem waiting to be great.

"A poem is a momentary stay against the confusion of the world"*
So, I think, must be a quarter mile race.
Time lives for hundredths of a second,
blocks out all else for the briefest time.
So, with creation of a poem.

*Robert Frost

Tyra Reyez   *Odessa*

THE BLUE HOUSE
(Frida Kahlo Museum)

Today at Frida's house tourists stand in line to see my sister's self-portraits. Impacted by her love letters and journals they become firsthand spectators around the ambulance, the bus crash, the handrail piercing her womb. But I have not come here to see sutures or Niñito Diego letters. I am here by accident. As absent-minded as stepping into the bath water with my socks on, I leave my house, pick up Frida's favorite cookies from the panadería, and arrive here at The Blue House as if she were still alive to receive me for our daily chat over a glass of horchata. She used to wait for me in the garden cupping raindrops in her palm as the thunder thrashed and cracked the sky. When I arrived trembling, she would laugh, "Cristina, storms make you jitter like a child," she would say, "think of the thunder as a deep-throated laugh."

Love notes to her husband show no struggle. Her long Tehuana dresses hide her polio leg. Her hair braided up in brilliant yellow ribbons and her bold earrings do not dangle a hint of pain. But after the accident and after each child disintegrated in her womb, Frida seemed like a parakeet in the house singing harder with its eyes maimed.

I wonder what the tourists think of her monkeys, fetuses, the color she gives pain. Every object in this house is Frida's dialogue with death. She did not shrink in its presence; she emasculated it, shaded it, and beautified it. Never has death lost so much its right to privacy. My sister was a joker; she shows you broken columns and a crushed spine, but she lived a life without punctures. I know her lovers' names, her vices and fetishes. She had getaway plans and excursions with Trotsky, her favorite bad words, and a doll's crib beside her bed. She took what was abhorrent to her soul and recycled it into a portrait on the wall.

These wooden spoons convince me Frida will return, serve dinner at the yellow table. I listen for the flow of her long dress to brush against me, the scent of her perfume to linger on my blouse. I look up at her self-portrait, wait for the expression to change. I imagine her watching me. She knows that as soon as I leave her house, I will go to the rotunda where a fire burns for the great men of Mexico. The words "Niñito Diego" repeat in my head as if it were some message I must smuggle to Diego's tomb. Perhaps she watches me as I walk down the stairs into her courtyard. She wants her message to travel safely in my steps. I choose my path carefully. I want a sequel at her balcony, where Frida's and Diego's shoes and hats are lifted and worn.

René Saldaña, Jr.   *Lawrenceville, GA*

OUR LOVE CUMBIA
(*para Kristina*)

This way
    and that
we dance
arms wrapped
around one
another
in our
love
    cumbia

Me pierdo
en el
    pa'lla
    y pa'ca
de nuestro amor

Thom D. Chesney   *Fort Worth*

BEHIND THE BOOKCASE

I don't expect you to believe this, but I have a cat named Wonderbread. That's right—same as the stuff kids love for peanut butter and jelly sandwiches. Now to me her name's not so strange as the way I acquired her. And that in and of itself is another story altogether. I was there, of course. It happened two summers ago.

A storm without lightning rumbled across the sky in the east toward Waxahachie, but on the edge of Midlothian, where we were, the rain was light. It brought up the oil and dirt that for four months had worked its way into the asphalt of Highway 287, making the road a shiny black ribbon. Each drop of water added to the greasy sheet that the drought had left beneath the road surface as a reminder of summer. Since June, the rains had never been heavy enough to clean the roads or revive the withered grass in the ditches.

My brother, Ryan Tenhold, rolled his window down and asked "Carver? You all right back there?"

"Yeah," I said, "just kick it up a gear or two. I don't feel like getting all wet." I pulled up the collar of my letter jacket as close to my ears as possible and leaned out from behind a mattress I'd been steadying against the gusty Texas wind. The pickup's bed wasn't wide enough to lay the mattress down, so Ryan, his friend Lonnie Maldano, and I had wedged it in next to a small desk and a bookcase. I lost the coin toss to Lonnie and had to ride in back to keep all of his furniture and junk from sliding around and falling out. We'd tied some of it down with a phone cord, but that wasn't likely to be enough. Since it was Ryan's truck, he naturally got to drive *and* flip the coin. There was no two out of three. I hopped in back and the journey began.

As we pulled onto the highway, the load shifted and nearly pinned my left leg between the floor and the wheel well. I yelled at Ryan to take it easy, but the truck windows were up now and a rapid-fire drum beat throbbed from the cab, nearly matching the rhythm of the Ford's rough engine. I had to pull my leg out of my boot and force my way back to the small open space near the tailgate. There I squatted on the balls of my feet, clinging to a small ridge of wood on the underside of the bookcase's bottom shelf. After a while I pretended I was water-skiing underhand, and every minute or so—as long as the road ran straight—I stood up a little and peeked out from behind the bookcase, hoping my brother wouldn't spot me and then swerve to try and scare the living crap out of me.

Ryan was very different from our father, Vern Tenhold. He had had eyes in the back of his head and would have spotted me the first time my red hair bobbed up from behind the bookcase. The truck would have come to a quick stop at the next intersection, and the driver's side door would have slammed shut almost before the parking brake was set. Right then I would know there was hell to pay.

"Was that you I saw sticking your head out at me with your rear end up off the truck bed?" Of course it had been. "Geez, Lou-eez!" My father never swore in front of us. "You must have been snorting pussy willows up your nose again and got your brain all clouded up. I don't know what's gotten into you today, Carver." He'd scratch his beard and grab my baseball cap by the brim and turn it around backwards. "You've been spending too much time around your brother, haven't you? Just keep your butt planted in the truck bed until we're in the driveway, son." Then my dad would have turned away, and I would have smiled.

I smiled like that now, doing the underhand water-ski and poking my head out to tick off my less-than-father-figure brother. I was sure that when Dad and Mom looked down on us now, that they would just as soon not have to watch. But today it was cloudy. That'd keep them from seeing this episode. Today I figured they could relax, and I could enjoy my little game.

A guitar wailed for a second and a beer bottle whizzed past my left ear, clinked once on the pavement and then spun onto the shoulder where it shattered. Then the music faded as quickly as it had burst from Ryan's window. Grabbing the bookcase with one hand and shielding my face with the other, I peeked out to my right, wondering if the two in front had discovered my game and a bottle from Lonnie would be flying by me next. I wanted to catch it and throw it back at him. Instead the music stopped in the middle of a song, and I heard Ryan shouting at Lonnie for playing the same thing over and over again. Before Lonnie could finish a sentence that started with the words "Eat my," a George Jones tape kicked in and overpowered Lonnie's whiny voice.

I wondered. How did Lonnie finish the phrase this time? "Eat my" what? Weenie? Big one? One-eyed trouser mouse? Lonnie had a list of 117 different words that you could say instead of . . . well, you can guess from the weenie reference. He kept the list in his wallet so he could add to it whenever he thought of a new word. I peered over the bookcase to see if Lonnie was writing anything down, but all I saw was the middle finger of Ryan's right hand pressed white against the back window. Lonnie had turned in his seat to smile back at me and make fish lips on the dirty glass. I defiantly returned my brother's hand signal and dropped out of sight once more.

Where the road curved and banked a little, the truck's balding tires gave in to momentum and slid across the sometimes solid, sometimes broken yellow line that separated one lane of traffic from the other. When the truck crossed that line, I had to crouch low, anticipating Ryan's abrupt move to the right. The rain had changed to a mist, and my face felt shiny and wet like the slick, oily road that was leading us to Waxahachie where we'd unload Lonnie's stuff and get him settled into his new apartment.

For now I'd have to sit and wait until the truck slowed to thirty-five miles per hour as we approached town. Fortunately, there was still time for one last ski run—one that took real guts, now that I'd been discovered. I wiped my hands one at a time on my socks, the only dry clothes left on my body. Then I reached for the bookshelf that was second from the top and raised myself up, facing the wind and mist head-on to yell, "You all suck! You suck—you suck—you suck!"

A red sedan passed by, and I dared to wave at it. The music still pounded inside the cab, and as far as I could tell Ryan and Lonnie, jamming with George, had yet to notice me. A blue pickup like ours passed, and I waved at it too, this time with my right hand. From then on I waved at cars with my left hand and everything else with my right, until I saw the big brown yacht making its way toward us.

My father once said that any car bigger than a Monte Carlo was a yacht and should be out on a lake, trolling for bass. This big brown Lincoln heading straight at us could have been rented out for dockside parties. It was a mammoth and deserved a two-handed salute.

So, as the Town Car passed the pick-up, I stretched my arms skyward into a wide V and waved my hands. I started to yell something, but a white flash no bigger than a bread bag was sucked from the passing car into my face, hitting me so hard that I flipped backward over the tailgate, my arms groping and flailing for the mattress that came along with me.

When we hit the ditch, I somehow landed on my back and mostly on the mattress, though my hands were skinned up pretty bad. I heard the pickup backing up and Ryan yelling all the while. So I lay there for a moment amongst the weeds and half a dozen or so spiders that had some real repair work do. And just then a bruised, disoriented, but nonetheless intact white Persian cat began licking at my left ear between taking little sniffs at the air. Alright, so she's a little bigger than a bread bag, but I named her Wonderbread anyway, which is what I started to say in the first place.

Frances Neidhardt   *Sherman*

ART CAPERS FRAMED AND FLOATING

Because so frequently brought home
By people visiting museums–perhaps
For overnight, sometimes for longer–
The question grows if painted people,
Given their infinite appearances as
Cardinals in crimson, roughnecks in
Blue, puttis prancing on clouds, nudes
Lolling on a couch, two-nosed people,
Stuffed shirts in the park, cadavers
Clothed in worms–if on gaining
Their release from frames these images
(or little nothings swimming paint-clad
From canvas to reality) must seek as
We unpainted do their own eventuality,
Relying, finally, on mystery for con-
clusion? Or whether they were finished
From the start? Or if as actors in a
Spinning world they live out one brief
Role and then another, birthing and
Dying to endless expectations, rotating
In a perpetuity of art lovers' dreams?

J. R. LeMaster   *Waco*

WHEN I STAND IN SILENCE

When I stand in silence
on the edge of my bath
the form of one first-born
comes to me in touches
of golden dawn, and then
I wander back to times
when all were here—at first
casting shadows upon
an unknown farmer's pond,
and then in gilt-edged pane
where I bathe white lilies
each morning when I rise
to face the day that comes
only in madmen's dreams,
the day, nevertheless,
that comes as all days must.
Forever I ponder
endless beachheads of time
searching for clues that once
they passed this way in all
their innocence—that once
they strayed too far from shore
in pursuit of the one
they thought to be first-born.
Tomorrow I will go,
again after bathing
the whitest of lilies,
and I will lie breathless
on a warm bed of sand
praying for the figure
taking another bath
inside the gilt-edged pane.

Carol Cullar   *Eagle Pass*

CONTAINERS

Chickens and dust are what it invariably came down to, she supposed. And there he stood doing the dance, the mindless step forward, the scratch backward that took him nowhere, then the cockeyed squint at the dust he'd stirred. Step, scratch, peer; but without progress. Sometimes he uncovered treasure, and a bug scuttled away or a shiny pebble gleamed, was lit upon with apparent delight and appropriate rejoicing, but mostly it was the dance, a stirring of the dust.

The rooster finished his business and with feigned squalk of terror fled across the track. She put the Rover in gear and finished the last eighty feet uninterrupted. The wait for the final cloud to settle was automatic. It didn't matter if the journey were eighty miles or eighty feet, there was always dust to settle at the end. She used the time to collect her thoughts and the woven bag for staples, settle her hat more firmly on her forehead, and wish for the ten thousandth time for something different.

But that was what had brought her here in the first place, wasn't it? She opened the door and accepted the last settling grains on her lips and across the bridge of her nose as a sacrament, the scorching sun as a benediction laid across her shoulders. If it sometimes seemed the blows of a mallet, so be it. It was what she'd chosen. The distance of her escape had folded back on itself, become irrelevant. Eight thousand or eighty. She was still left with the chickens and the dust. The half century in between, a mere flicker.

The Bejan waiting in the depths of the store greeted her with a flash of pleasure.

"Good morning, Matthew Otunga! Your family is well? N'tala has not been in school this week." She leveled a patient gaze.

Matthew's smile grew, and he stood even taller. "N'tala helps her mother with the new child. She returns to school next week. Teacher, you have a letter arrive here two days ago from Tex-as!" He placed the crumpled envelope into her hand and watched with reluctance as she slipped it into the pocket of her smock.

She turned her back and stared into the bins of produce, potatoes slipping down just a bit from their once neat stacks to mingle with the eggplants, the beans and lentils overlapping, a sifting of dust over everything; borders and demarcations shifting, blurring. The heat from outside suddenly overwhelmed.

She searched for the scoop, but found the squares of paper first. With fingers that did not tremble, she rolled a deft cone and after a search, located the tool. Although they had not been on her list, she began tumping lentils into the receptacle. A few beans intermingled.

She handed the package to Matthew to weigh and watched his fingers complete the twist and tuck flap that sealed the container and had always escaped her attempts to learn. She moved to the next group of bins to lift a small clay salt dish, tip it into the waiting paper cone stacked at a tilt and end buried beside the bowl's imprint. Step, scoop, examine. Step, scoop, examine. She pulled the basket from out her bag and said, "Twelve eggs should be enough, Matthew."

Her fingers noticed the containers, their textures beneath her roughened fingertips, the basket—worn and serviceable from the hands of N'tala or her mother, paper—crinkled, recycled from an Arabic newspaper, the clay bowl—close to home and only slightly changed, compressed from the dust outside, the metal scoop from far away—warm, with just a bit of grit dulling its surface. Containers designed for specific tasks, their contents mixed.

Her eye caught the rustle of feathers through the opened doorway. "Matthew, how much for that young rooster in the yard?"

Greg Young   *Abilene*

EXAM

Dr. Winston-Kennedy snaps a latex glove
against her wrist like a rubber band. She tells me to relax.
If only her face did not remind me of Miss Landenberg
who used to read poems in class, poems that boy like me
were not supposed to like. I remember the day Coach Mann
burst in, proposed to her in front of class in his green
coaching shorts, on his hairy little knees. He called her Inga.

A man should never wear a gown,
much less a gown that leaves his butt exposed to air.
Wouldn't it be better to be naked, to be stretched out
on a table like a specimen she probes with cold,
sterile instruments clinking on a stainless steel tray?
Then she would not talk to me as if we were playing cards.
She would not ask about the Series, who I'm pulling for.
She would not mix chatter with statistics, my EKG,
my waist-to-hip ratio, my need for yearly exams.

I'll bet Coach Mann never had yearly exams. He went
the way he wanted to, bottom of the ninth, May afternoon,
beside the pitcher's mound. He grabbed his chest, collapsed.
Inga ran out to him, cradled his head, pleaded for help,
Paramedics arrived, tried to beat the life back into him,
loaded his body on a stretcher, carried him off the field.
Word spread from the field, to the dugout, to the bleachers...

Bob McCranie   *Carrollton*

TESTING THE SIRENS

for Danny Lusk

Every Wednesday at noon they wail,
long and loud over the city,
the warnings of destruction, imminent and final.
Eating lunch outside it's amazing
how clear the siren sounds
throwing its voice hard against the Fall.
I'm thinking, Danny, over pasta, how futile it is–by the time
you catch their cry in the wind, the storm is already upon you,
the bruised sky, God's long winding down
from heaven to earth, touching and destroying
everything loved. When I was young, Mom made us hide
deep and quiet in the bare concrete cellar every time the sky got dark—
and she was right.

It's been 10 years now since the sirens started to wail. Ten years
living under the blood gun. I saw once how a twister drove
a 2x4 through the trunk of a 40 year old Elm tree as if it were putty.
This is where we belonged, Danny, here under the clear sky
hearing the sirens for what they really are, the God call, the mother cry,
knowing their voices fully before love and destruction came crashing down.

Carol J. Rhodes   *Houston*

DUMPSTER AFTER DARK

Searching
through mounds of trash
for chicken bones
with gristled joints he could gnaw
or the prize of a half-eaten biscuit,
the old man,
in clothes oiled slick with dirt,
scared away
two starving cats
who wanted *his* dinner.

Chuck Etheridge   *Abilene*

GIMME A HEAD WITH HAIR . . .

High school really began for me when I started to let my hair grow out.

Like most of the other big events that happened to me during high school, my big change started by accident. One day, after school, I was staring at myself in the mirror, looking for zits. I took a few minutes to hate my bright red hair, because it made me look so different from everyone else.

I began to wonder what my hair would look like if I combed it differently.

I usually parted it on the side, so I tried combing it straight forward, giving myself bangs. Pretty dorky, very little kiddish, and my bangs were crooked, anyway.

Then I tried parting it on the left, but that was no change—just a mirror image of the way I usually looked. Combing it straight back did nothing—it just stuck out in all directions. If I had wanted to look like that famous dead old science guy I'd heard of called Arthur or Albert Einstein (I never could get the name right), I would have gone with that look, but I was trying to get past a reputation badly sullied by straight 'A's' and a stint of cello playing.

Wait a minute, I thought. The college guys I'd seen, or a lot of them, any-way, parted their hair in the middle. So I tried that, starting at the front and working my way back, brushing one side and then the other. It was harder than I thought it was gonna be, and it took me at least a million tries before I got the part halfway straight.

Dorkhood at a higher level. I looked like one of those barbershop singer guys I sometimes saw on TV variety shows. I grabbed a folded-up towel, holding it over my heart the way those barbershop fellas held their straw hats, and started belting out, "You'll look sweet . . .upaaaaawn the seat . . . " Going for the big finale, I spread my arms and sang, "Of a bicycle built for TWOOOOO!"

I busted out laughing. My face turned red when I did, making the freckles really stand out.

"Peter Laurence Talbott, what are you doing in there?" came the voice from the other side of the door.

"Uh, nothing, Mom."

"What's all that noise?"

"Nothing."

"You've been in there fifteen minutes. You can't be doing nothing."

Mom was in one of her Sergeant Joe Friday moods, interrogating me. This usually happened when one of her work friends told her something horrible about one of their kids, like they'd brought home bad grades or had gotten caught with marijuana—two things that seemed to always go together in my mother's mind.

"I'm combing my hair, Mom."

"Well, hurry up, son. Other people need to use that bathroom."

"I'll come right out if you need to go, Mom."

"I don't need to go. But I might sometime, so you better hurry up."

The weird part was I always understood her when she said things like that. "Sure, Mom. Be right out."

Her departing voice called out, "Walter! I think he's started masturbating."

I wasn't entirely sure what the word meant, but it sounded bad. I shrugged and started combing the sides of my hair, for the first time combing down instead of back. To my surprise, my hair had grown out 'til it was just long enough to barely cover the tip of my ears.

Now the part in the middle looked different. I didn't look like a Barber Shop Quartet Guy. I looked like a College Guy. I . . .

"Get out of there THIS INSTANT!" Dad's voice boomed.

I dropped the comb and scooted right out of there.

Then I went into the kitchen, and, hoping to avoid further trouble, I said, "Uh, Mom, can I help with dinner?"

"Sure, Pete," she said, not turning around "Could you peel three potatoes?"

"Okay. I mean, yes, ma'am." I'd been forgetting the 'ma'am' part recently. She didn't mind so much, but Dad went totally nutso when I forgot and said I was 'being disrespectful,' and I figured he might be listening. I fished three potatoes out of the pantry, then rooted around the gunk drawer until I found the potato peeler.

As I stood over the trash can peeling so the bits of skin went into the bin, I asked, "Mom, what's masturbation?"

She dropped whatever it was she was holding. It fell in the sink. It broke. It must have been a plate of something. The back of her neck got real red, real fast.

"Pete, it's . . ." she turned around. "AAAAAAHHHHH!" she screamed. "AAAAAAAAHH!"

That made me cut myself with the potato peeler, so I started screaming "AAAH, AAAH!" too. Let me tell you, it's pretty hard to cut yourself with a potato peeler, but when you do, it hurts, big-time.

So Mom's screaming for some unknown reason and I'm screaming because I've got blood gushing out all over three potatoes, so Dad charges into the room and says, "What the hell's going on in here?"

"I cut my hand."

Mom just pointed at me. I still didn't know what made her scream, but I was more worried about my hand.

"Let's get it cleaned up, son." Dad was occasionally good in a crisis. He took my hand and examined it. "That's pretty nasty." He led me by the hand past Mom and over toward the sink and ran water on it.

"Walter. Waaaaallll-terrrrr!" Mom wailed. "Look at him!"

"Darling," Dad said, matter-of-factly. "It's just a cut. No one has ever been fatally injured by a potato peeler." By this time, he'd rinsed my hand and was drying it off with a paper towel.

"No," sobbed Mom. "Look at his hair!"

They'd rushed me out of the bathroom so quick I'd clean forgotten about my new 'do. I was busted.

"I hadn't noticed," he said. "Looks fine."

Sometimes my father totally shocked me. Usually he was a drill sergeant having a bad day, but there were these occasional flashes of patience and kindness. I was so used to Drill Sergeant that it always surprised me when Patient Guy popped up out of nowhere. I grinned at him. He put a Band-Aid on my hand.

"Good as new," he said.

"But look at it," she hissed, her teeth clenched.

"What about it?"

"It's long. It's over his ears."

"It's shorter than what most of the boys up at the college are wearing, Ann. And probably shorter than most of the other kids I've seen over at Central High."

Whoa. Dad standing up for me was virgin territory. If I'd been smart, I would have retreated to my room, claiming homework or a sudden attack of yellow fever. But I just stood there, watching, fascinated.

"You know what happened to the Morris boy. He started wearing his hair long, and the next thing we heard, he was arrested for drugs."

"I know that, dear. But the hair didn't make him do drugs."

"But it's the first step!" Mom looked panicked.

"Son," Dad said, turning calmly to me. "I think you'd best go to your room. We'll call you when dinner's ready."

"Uh, yes sir." I got out of there, but I moved slowly. It was the train wreck thing again—I didn't want to watch my parents fight, but I didn't want to miss it, either.

I went to my room, shut my door, sat down, and began picking out a Ricardo Valenzuela tune, the one he'd written about a girl he liked, the one he'd recorded under the name Ritchie Valens. "I had a girl . . . . Donna was her name . ."

Then I stopped. "I had a girl . . . Letty was her name . . ." I grinned shyly at the thought, even though I was alone. No one, and I mean no one, knew about my crush on Leticia Benevídez. Then I kept on, and since my voice had changed, I could do the lower "Doe doe doe doe" parts real good.

About half an hour later, Dad came and got me. Mom was sitting at the kitchen table, arms crossed, pointedly not looking at Dad, or me.

"Your Mother has decided we ought to go and pick up something for dinner. Would you like to come?"

Sometimes you know when a question is an order. "Sure, dad."

"Let's go."

On our way to Der Wienerschnitzel, the fast-food place closest to the house, Dad explained to me that they'd "decided to let me wear my hair however I wanted to."

"Thanks, Dad."

He smiled, something I rarely saw. "You're welcome, son."

It was the high point of father-son relations in my teen years.

Chris Ellery   *San Angelo*

INHERITANCE

I have inherited my father's pants,
red flannel plaid, soft for sleeping.
I stole them from his closet
when my brothers weren't looking.
A week after his death
it is the end of winter in Texas.
Let me see where I can walk to in these pants.
Past the bedroom where my son is
saying in his sleep Dad Dad.
Out of the house and into the yard.
There are wild flowers, weeds really,
the kind that ruins grass.
For the first time
I see how beautiful they are.
Down Cleveland Street, past
the persimmon tree and the baseball field,
across the stone bridge,
tadpoles in the creek, to Bramble Park.
He coaxed me from my fear
to the top of the big slide
where gravity grabbed me and I felt
freedom
for the first time.
Out Genoa Road to the lake
where he took me fishing
for the first time.
He wasn't much of a fisherman.
We never caught anything but joy.
You can only catch that by jumping in,
letting it swallow you for three days.
It belches you back up on the shore
with its dirty sand, stone, and bare
crucifix branches.
But you're not the same.

Jackie Pelham   *Houston*

THE SAMARITAN

What else was I to do? What would you have done?

It was the final leg of a successful trip, a retreat to the Adirondacks, cold and cleansing, inspiring. And so, in the overloaded plane, the seats so close you could feel the pulsebeat of the person beside you, I sat listening to the child crying in the rear, out of control, trying to tell the mother, begging the mother for comfort. The woman was a worn out traveler, from where I did not know, but foreign, yes, obviously foreign. The cry was universal, fear, hunger, pain.

As I rose and jostled back, I understood the consternation, the need for relief in the woman's face, knew in the niggling far reaches of my mind that the sound of the infant was, after all, different. But I, feeling pity as any compassionate person might, went to the mother, stooped over, smiled and held out my arms for the baby, if only to quiet the cry, to give the woman relief. And didn't I, at this point in my life, have the time to do good deeds? The gratitude I saw there encouraged and I cradled the baby, gazed at its pale lips drawn back in a grimace, stared into dark-brown squinted eyes, and I knew instinctively they were not the eyes of a well child, its arms flailing wildly, tiny fingers clutching at me, sharp papery nails pricking my arms, the rancid odor familiar. I held the soiled bundle close, cooed, rocked back and forth as I had rocked my own children many years before, until finally exhausted the baby quieted and dozed fitfully.

In the closeness, the odor of travelers' bodies stifled and I dared not breathe. Embarrassed, I looked past their tired faces, settling only on the infant's face, pained even in sleep. It came to me that I had seen the same expression somewhere before, but where? Worrisome thing, not to remember.

And then the scene erupted so vivid, I clenched my eyes to fling it from my mind. The Good Samaritan trip to Africa last summer, the natives lying in a makeshift hospital that was only a tent with no netting, emaciated bodies buzzed by flies, boils and sores excreting yellow pus, the smell rancid as the child's smell was rancid.

The disease's name flashed hot and searing to my brain, and in horror, I staggered back in the aisle, away from the woman, the child falling from my arms like a hot-iron, burning, contagious, incurable.

Michael Goins   *Austin*

FIRST IMPRESSIONS

It was almost two hours before the family stopped and offered me a ride, and if it hadn't been for the uniform, I don't think they'd have stopped then.

"Too much crap goin' on, ya know?" said the father. He leaned toward me to check out the GI haircut and the fresh pressed uniform. "Throw your duffel in the back and climb in. Where ya headed?"

"Home." The heavy bag slipped off my shoulder. I shoved it into the back seat, climbed in behind it, and slammed the heavy door. "I'm headed home."

"Carpenter," he said, reaching over the vinyl back of the seat and extending a hand. "Ben Carpenter. This here's my wife, Callie."

When I didn't offer a name, he looked at the military nametag on my uniform pocket. "Garcia?"

"Yeah. That's it. Garcia. Billy Garcia."

"That's an odd name, don't you think so Ben?"

"No worse than Callie Carpenter, I reckon," he said with a smile.

"You don't look Mexican." She turned back to her husband. "Does he Ben? He don't look Mexican at all. Especially with that red hair and all them freckles."

"Leave the boy alone, Callie. For God's sake."

I silently slide the knife open, and realized for the first time I should have killed the white boy instead of the Mexican. I wouldn't make that mistake again.

Jerry Hamby   *Houston*

ABIQUIU

O'Keeffe bought the house for its black door,
hundred-year-old timber, distilled
on canvas, stripped to color, line, and form,
like hollyhock, jimsonweed, crows, ladders, and bones.
She bought the house for its adobe walls and earthen
floors, furnished it with plywood and muslin.
At night she climbed the roof and watched
stars through boughs of tamarisk.
By day she hiked the Black Place, the White Place,
painted, searched for desert bones; she walked
along the Chama, filling pockets with river rocks.
Eyesight failing, she carried stones
from window sill to garden wall and turned them
in hand, learning line and form.
With a single stroke of brown across
white canvas, she painted the winter road
as ribbon, winding down from the Red Hills
and Cerro Pedernal, arcing from Abiquiu to Santa Fe.

Susann Gipson **Waco**

THE LILY POND

When Maria Ordoñes Castillo had a vision of the Virgin Mary in the lily pond behind the old Santa Fe train station, she told her sister Consuela because she always told Consuela everything. Consuela listened to Maria's stories with tears and embraces because she loved her and because of what Maria had suffered at the hands of her husband. Nevertheless, Consuela, having studied psychology at the community college in Albuquerque, knew that Maria was a lunatic, and she knew that now Maria was more crazy than ever and was beginning to have hallucinations. So Consuela told her husband Hugo, who was a smart businessman with a chain of very successful dry cleaning outlets, that something had to be done about Maria.

Hugo listened with some interest to the story of Mary's appearance among the lily pads. Hugo's mother had been a Texas Baptist, and he did not believe that the Virgin Mary ever returned to earth, no matter how earnestly she might be entreated to do so by the simple New Mexicans that Maria and Consuela had grown up among. Mary's work, he devoutly believed, had been completed when she gave birth to her Son, who brought true salvation to all the lost souls who needed only to confess openly that he had so done, as he had explained to Connie when he introduced her to his church that was famous for having displayed the first neon cross in New Mexico. But having made a good profit on key chains and small statues of Our Lady of Guadalupe at the check out stands in his dry cleaners, Hugo thought that a vision of Mother Mary might have lucrative possibilities.

Secretly, Hugo thought that Connie's faith in psychology was as naive as Maria's faith in the Virgin, but he agreed that Maria was a lunatic. For what other reason could she have chosen to live in an old cinder block house on a dirt road, raising chickens, when she could have had a smart apartment in Albuquerque and worked in one of his dry cleaning outlets. Even leaving her husband Hank, he thought, was impractical. What if he did rough her up a little when he got too drunk? Connie always let her in, and Hank made very good money. How could an ignorant woman, alone, hope to make a living babysitting and selling eggs? Connie, thank God, was just the opposite of Maria. A great wife and mother, she made ten dollars seem like a hundred.

The problem with Maria, the family all agreed, was caused by her grandmother, Lupe, who had chosen to live with her husband on a Navajo reservation. Connie and Maria's mother had insisted that English only be spoken in her home, and she taught her children to value education, hard work, and success. The only hope for Latinos, she was persuaded, was to join the business world of the greater community, as she called the Anglos in Albuquerque and Santa Fe. But Grandmother Lupe had married a Navajo and wore old fashioned, long dresses and moccasins well into the seventies, when nearly everyone else, even on the reservation, was wearing jeans and tee shirts everywhere except tourist fairs and flea markets. After years of sullen refusal to speak more than an essential word or two to her daughter and grandchildren, she developed an intense bond with Maria, surprising everyone because Maria had blue-gray eyes. Stringing ristras and corn beads, she told Maria stories about her childhood in the Jicarrilla Mountains and about the early New Mexican Indians and the Kachinas. She gave Maria a silver ring inlaid with a rainbow man for a graduation present.

So when it was time for Maria to follow Connie to college, she was already ruined. Earning passing grades only in Freshman Composition and American History, she neglected to turn in her homework for Business Math; and eighties on the tests did not offset zeros on the daily work. She dropped the rest of her courses after mid-term, so they were also recorded as "F's". Consequently, the family was quite relieved when Hank Waller, who owned a popular hamburger stand, asked her to marry him. And Maria, who loved Connie's children and offered to baby sit almost every evening, had seemed radiantly happy whenever he stopped by, hamburgers in hand, to spend the evening with her while she watched the children. Connie said she would be a beautiful bride and a wonderful mother, and only Grandmother Lupe said nothing, watching Maria and watching Hank with dry, piercing eyes.

The anticipated children never came, and Maria's radiance dimmed as her reliance on heavy makeup increased. On Christmas Eve, two years and eleven months after her marriage, she hid in the Garcia's barn, hollow eyed and desperate, and refused to speak to anyone who said she should try "to work things out with Hank." Finally, even Hugo felt relieved when Hank agreed to a divorce. No one had thought he would give her up so easily. For her part, Maria gave him everything, asking only for her collection of family photographs.

It was the Garcias who gave Maria the small house on a half acre of caleche, in exchange for cooking for their family and caring for their children two or three evenings a week. Maria loved her home, loved the solitude in the Rio Grande country. She built a large pen for her chickens, which she refused to kill for meat, using them only for fresh eggs to be given to her family and friends and to be sold in the farmers' market. She also grew corn, tomatoes, and a few other vegetables for her own use and to supplement the chicken feed she bought at a seed store. Every evening, after the children were asleep and the Garcias were home for the night, she walked with a pied greyhound that she had found, starving and sore footed, limping along the highway toward Albuquerque.

She had discovered the lily pond by following the dog around the old train station. The pond was part of an abandoned garden that had once been filled with tables where travelers could stop for a drink or for dinner, shop for Indian jewelry, or simply walk for a few minutes, dropping pennies into the pond in hopes that their wishes would be granted. Several large goldfish had survived, and they swirled around her hands in a joyful dance when she scattered the

same feed for them that she gave her chickens. She cleared the debris from the bottom of the pond, washed the hand painted tiles that lined its sides and edges, and pulled the weeds, transforming the old ruin into a lovely retreat. Prickly pear and yucca had replaced the original flowers giving the garden a timeless quality that greatly appealed to Maria's sensibility. She would sit, listening to music and laughter coming from a nearby tavern and watching the reflection of the bright, New Mexican sky turn red, then orange, and finally, blue black.

Occasionally, if they had no one to spend the night with, Nancy and Monique, who worked at The Cantina, would stop at Maria's pond, and the three unlikely friends would talk for hours at a time. The Cantina was frequented mostly by local Latinos, and occasionally by Anglos from Albuquerque who had heard that Nancy and Monique would go out with anyone, a rumor that was not entirely false, especially since the local Latinos would not have any thing to do with them, fearing the diseases that Albuquerque Gringos were known for. Usually, the locals ignored the outsiders, and both ignored a quiet blond man who came every Saturday night to drink Dos Eques until he could just limp to his pick up, where he slept until some undetermined time in the early morning when he drove away. Nancy and Monique liked to flirt with him, taking bets on who would get him to spend the night first, but he treated them with distant politeness, leaving modest tips when he was not too drunk.

So the Cantina crowd were surprised when he started a fight with a large Marine, who become obnoxious when Monique refused to dance with him. They were not surprised when the Marine beat him unmercifully, but after the fight, they ignored him with a new degree of respect. The poolside conversations were merrier because Nancy could always make Monique giggle by lowering her voice and saying "The lady doesn't want to dance."

When he bought the vacant land at the end of Maria's street and placed a trailer there, everyone but Maria thought she was much safer with him in the neighborhood. He was safer, she quipped, walking home from The Cantina, instead of driving.

At first, Maria resented having the road, which she had begun to think of as her own, inhabited by someone else. Nancy's report that he had been a sniper in Viet Nam who had not adjusted well after the war did not make her feel more neighborly. Her attitude softened, however, when he placed a large terra cotta pot of salmon colored geraniums in front of his house. Later, when he began to share the hot dogs that he cooked on a small outdoor grill with her greyhound, who usually remained well out of arm's reach of everyone except Maria, she started leaving two or three fresh eggs by his door, early every morning before he woke up.

Maria's routine of caring for her chickens, cooking for the Garcia's, long walks, and longer conversations beside her beloved pond grew increasingly comfortable, so she felt uneasy when Hugo persuaded Consuela to take her to see a priest about her vision of the lady in the pond. The priest, however, who had never heard of Mary's appearing among goldfish and lilies, was skeptical that a true miracle had occurred. Maria agreed that, although she had seen a woman's image among the lilies, it did not seem very miraculous. The priest advised Consuela to permit Mary to continue her ascetic life, explaining that she did not pose a threat either to herself or to others. So Maria seemed destined to live in simple contentment. That was before a rattlesnake found its way to Maria's dirt road.

Maria had suspected a snake was present when three of her chicks disappeared. She bought some fine gage wire and reinforced the perimeters of her pen, and kept a wary eye in the evening when she walked. A rat snake, she reasoned, did more good than harm, and she welcomed the help in protecting her chicken food from mice. But when she found her greyhound, swollen and acutely ill, lying near the road in front of her house, she knew it was a rattlesnake.

Grateful for a neighbor with a pick up, she asked him to take her and the greyhound to a veterinarian. Maria intended to tie a scarf around the dog's muzzle, but before Maria could catch up with him, he had scooped the long legged dog in his arms and settled him on a blanket in the space behind his seat in the pickup. Driving to the clinic, he explained that his name was Joe McIntyre; he had lived in Seattle, but he preferred the climate in New Mexico. He could live on disability pay because of his leg that had been hit with shrapnel. He was lucky; it got him out of Nam. He had wanted to be a teacher, but he had lost the patience to work with children. He had been married, but his marriage had not worked out. Maria noticed silver intermixed with the blond in his hair, and deep lines on his face that made him look older than he had seemed from a distance. Holding the door to the clinic open, while Joe carried the hound from the truck, she watched tears puddle under his eyes, trickle down the sides of his nose, and down the lines above his mouth.

The Veterinarian wanted to keep Maria's greyhound for a few days, so Joe promised a ride and help getting him home. As a thank you present, Maria gave him a flashlight to use at night when he walked to and from The Cantina. The next afternoon, he built a large doghouse and filled it with hay, so the hound would have a comfortable place to convalesce.

"I can't believe you haven't given him a name," he complained, tacking a blanket across the door to keep out the chilly evening breezes.

That evening, Maria had almost fallen asleep when she heard the noise, and the gun. Running outside, she saw Joe shooting the snake repeatedly.

"You only have to kill it once," she said, reaching for the spent pistol, then putting her arm around his waist when she saw his eyes.

Inside, warming a pan of apple cider with cloves and cinnamon, she asked, "Tell me what happened in Viet Nam," but he drank the cider silently, thanked her, and walked back to his trailer.

On Saturday morning, Joe drove Maria to the clinic to pick up the greyhound, which became excited at the sight of Maria. "He might have a scar, and a little tissue damage in his back leg," the veterinarian explained, " but he should recover very well. Fortunately, he is a very fast runner, and the snake hit his behind. A bite in the chest would have been more dangerous."

The hound liked his straw bed, and Joe seemed to linger, making certain that he was comfortable, until Maria suggested that he walk with her that evening, offering to show him the lily pond she had found.

"Come get me, whenever you're ready," he answered, complicating Maria's simple life.

When she knocked at his door, Joe invited her in, so he could put on boots and a jacket. He opened his refrigerator, reached for a Seven Up, and poured it in a plastic glass for her. To her surprise, there was no beer in the refrigerator, just Seven Up, a carton of milk, and the morning's fresh eggs. In his living room, there were three paintings of the mesas between Albuquerque and Santa Fe and an unfinished sketch of Maria's greyhound.

"You can name him," she said, when he stepped out of his bedroom, jacket in hand.

Watching the sky's colorful transformation in Maria's pond, Joe said that he was no good as a husband. He couldn't sleep well because he dreamed, nearly every night, that he was running, his best friend dying in his arms, through a jungle exploding into orange flames all around him. He would also leave home for weeks at a time to camp in the mountains. At his wife's insistence, he checked into a veteran's hospital, but he found their drugs addictive, and the dream, if anything, became more intense. Finally, his wife left him, saying that if he would not work to support them, she had to be able to sleep at night, so she could. He couldn't blame her for leaving. Maria said she had not been able to sleep well when she was married, either.

Joe, Maria, and the nameless greyhound walked together nearly every evening. The Garcia children giggled at him because he and the greyhound walked with a similar limp. Maria glared at them, but Joe, not quite catching the joke, smiled indulgently. He also joined the late night talks with Nancy and Monique, though Monique nearly ruined the first evening by laughing when she recognized who he was. He built small fires to keep the garden by the pond warm enough that the four friends were able to continue their late night visits through the winter. Joe continued to stop at The Cantina on Saturday nights, but he drank less and left earlier.

On Christmas Eve, watching the candles Maria and Nancy had placed along the edge of the pond, Joe named the greyhound Dream Runner. His dream of the burning jungle in Viet Nam had changed. His friend, this time, was alive when they were loaded on the helicopter, and he said "Thank You," very clearly. Then Joe noticed that the greyhound had also been running with him in the dream, and was on the helicopter. He looked down on the jungle from the air, and watched the burning trees become "smaller and smaller as the helicopter flew farther and farther away from them."

A few months later, Nancy married one of the men from Albuquerque whom she had met at The Cantina; and Monique, whose real name turned out to be Dolores, decided to rejoin her family, who had moved to Lubbock. When the days began to lengthen, and tiny buds appeared on the lilacs growing along the Garcia's fence, Maria started to wear lighter sweaters, and Joe noticed that she was gaining weight.

That evening, while Maria was feeding the goldfish, the lady in the pond appeared again, looking directly into her eyes. Then she saw a man with silver hair rising from the depths of the pond. Turning away from the pond, she saw a simple silver ring in Joe's hand.

"I want to name your child, too," he said, slipping the ring on her finger.

"I guess we can always sleep in separate houses, if we have to," she answered, as golden fish scattered translucent, round eggs on the blue green tiles among the shadows under green lily leaves and swelling pink buds.

Tony Clark   *Georgetown*

MY WIFE AMONG THE APACHES

A dreadful note jarred Linda from sleep
one night when she lived at San Carlos.
Peering out a window, she saw
in her porch light's stark aura
a small gray owl perched
on a branch of thorny mesquite.
With round eyes locked
on hers, it hooted once more.

On the Rez, according to her students,
the owl's a foreteller of death.
At school next day, Linda made haste
to question a colleague who would know.

The woman frowned at first,
then a shy smile shaped her auburn face
and her coal-dark eyes grew bright.
You don't need to worry, she said:
When the owl brings that kind
of news, it will speak Apache.

Al Haley *Abilene*

A STRANGER SEARCHES FOR FREE AIR ON A BLUSTERY DAY IN SWEETWATER, TEXAS

The wind, the wind. And on top of that the rear right is sagging when he comes off the highway. This station wants three quarters popped into the machine. Next bandit rates a buck for their miracle device out behind the pumps next to a cow pasture. The strongest gusts yet buffet the side of the car and an isosceles-shaped piece of cardboard floats over the hood like a prehistoric bird on the prowl for lizards. Where are the cows today? He's an Easterner, dressed in black. Can't figure it. Bovines must have been blown cudless to Ft. Worth. He keeps on driving, a man with a veined map but not a mission except to get his fine sedan through the wide state of Texas as fast as someone trying to escape an endless mall parking lot in time for dinner. Past a dozen steeple-free churches and rampant signs for some unsavory thing called "Rattlesnake Roundup!" The VFW Post is having a pancake breakfast. Who eats pancakes anymore? Can anyone afford real, tongue satisfying maple syrup with what's happening to the hardwoods in New England? And what about VDW, veterans of domestic wars? Finally, where the star of the American road has fallen off the overhead sign, *bingo*, got it. Unscrew the tire valve, couple the ball head to the stem while the wind is all momentum and that dull *thump, thump* against the eardrums. He dispenses satisfying squirts and the tire goes up like a fat man lazily rising from a chair. In the background, with great dignity, an aluminum can rolls to the curb, bumps over, wallows into the street and keeps going. Soon, it is out of sight behind a ragged line of mesquite, a reminder that this is not just any windy day. He is witness to the Pepsi that is making its way from sea to shining sea. That bold cylinder knows that the journey of many miles begins with the breath of someone larger than ourselves saying rock on out of here and go precisely where? Surely it is a split-tongue mystery to ponder in the rearview mirror as he reacquires highway speed, assisted by the mighty tailwind that is so kind to mileage, moods, and a man's wandering ways. The wind, the wind. Breathing gusty regret upon fresh drops of oil, the dibs and dabs of internal combustion, he has left behind on the pavements of Sweetwater, Texas.

Jefrrey DeLotto   *Fort Worth*

A MORNING START, SAGE CREEK RANCH

We swung open the ringing gate across the road,
Looking onto a green-swathed meadow between
A levee on the Little Missouri and an outcropping
Of Bentonite and flint, waded into drenched dawn
Grass and shook buckets rattling with oats, calling,
"Here, Spot—C'mon here Susie Q, Roanie Baloney,
B.J., Beeg, here boy," rope halters draped around
Our necks, until Sue and then Spot, and then the
Whole remuda of a dozen horses streamed through
The gate toward the corral.

Picking our four and four more, too, for the afternoon,
We turned the rest back into the mist that still hung
In patches ankle-deep in the hollows.

And as we brushed our mounts, their muscles quivering
Under the curry bristles, bank upon bank of scents rolled
Through the barn, first old hay and the delicate nut-like
Toast of oats poured into shallow troughs, scrabbled
Up by massaging velvet lips, followed by the rhythmical
Crunch of powerful teeth busying the horses as we brushed.
Soon there followed the dropping of dung, steaming in strong-
Scented piles, bright green as fresh pesto, the path so clear
And clean from pasture grass to tight belly to slowly closing
Sphincter ring, the broad aluminum shovel tossing it out
Onto the pile to lard the garden loam for finger-thick
Asparagus to thrust through, Freudian green and strong.
Next the blankets, upended since last their use had
Wet them on a ride, were balanced on the broad
Brushed backs, the sweat wool smell pushed aside
By that of harness leather and oily soap as saddles
Were swung up into place, lifted, twisted, and settled
Again, the cinch straps and belly bands tightened.

We led the horses, Sue, Spot, B.J., and Roany, out
Into the chill sunlight, tightened cinches, slapped the
Older mare Sue trying to swell her stomach for a
Slacker ride, and swung up, heading down the road's
Shoulder, for the Red House Pasture and some thirty
Pairs of heifers and calves to gather by noon.
And this the start of each day.

Chip Dameron   *Brownsville*

CYBERSCRIBING IN COWTOWN

On a clear day you can hear
them, south of the stockyards:
academic cowpokes, milling about
in an air conditioned holding pen
downtown, MOOing through a rattle
of keystrokes, swapping GUI tales
at coffee breaks, waiting for
the Prophets of Rock to mount
the makeshift stage and trade
hot licks for hot links to every
dancer's virtual past, where Lennon
might befriend the duke of URL.

C. Prudence Arceneaux   *Austin*

DIRT

I am not a gardener, grubber of plants,
shifting of soil. My nails clean,
I stopped kneeling years before I reached
this age. If you ask, I can tell a food seed
from a pretty one. Clarify that TOMATO is fruit.
Tell you: When the red hibiscus sits crushed in your hand,
it smells of blood. The hammerhead worm
tosses its head wetly when cut with a spade. A crooked
row means death for someone. Shit produces the best foundation.
A tree can live around the rot at its base, but dies
in the beauty of mistletoe. Poisoned grass returns as weeds,
mutates to flowers. Blue morning glories will cover your garden.
Beautiful, but chokes your roses.

All this I learned on my knees, from my father,
my teacher, beer in one hand, the other browner in dirt:

That the dog will follow and proof your work. That, here,
the frost will come back and kill your grapes,
no matter what. That squirrels stockpile,
even when there is no need.

Robert A. Ayres   *Austin*

BERSERK

The dog's berserk —
must be a mouse
in the cast iron furnace,
brittle, honeycombed
Alhambra window, where winter
the blue-fire burns.

I could strike a match,
turn on the gas.
See how this poem could end?

Outside, it's raining.
The fat drops of summer.

David Breeden   *Kerrville*

FOLKS IS LIKE THAT

Silas waited patiently in the dark. Crouched amongst the roots of a huge white oak, he rubbed his trigger finger against the reassuring bark of roots that had long ago washed out of the ground and fought to become just another piece of the woods. Still, for all its trying, the bark wasn't quite right somehow, not proper tree bark. It had stretched into tiny ovals, like alligator skin. Silas saw an alligator once, in town, made into a lady's purse.

Sooner or later that old man would have to come out. Sooner or later, every man goes to the outhouse. That much is clear. And when he does.... Well, sometimes there's somebody waiting for him. That much is clear too. Silas's daddy always taught him that: You really want to find somebody, you wait out by his outhouse. He'll be there sooner or later. Folks is like that.

Silas wondered why, when you stay still, really still, you've got so many itches. Silas had little itches everywhere. And it wasn't mosquitoes, either. Fall had come on, and the first frost, and nearly the whole woods lay as dead as his daddy. Pretty near, anyhow. A hoot owl was out. A whippoorwill. Seems like maybe he'd heard a rabbit four or so yards off. Not much alive. Hard to tell. Hard to hear: A big rain had come and the high water bashed against rocks down in the ravine.

Silas rubbed his trigger finger down the blue, pitted barrel of his twelve gauge. Prettiest weapon ever made, a single-shot twelve gauge. Simple. God's own weapon, a break-open twelve gauge. A man could kill just about anything first time with one of these, and if he didn't, another shell was in before you could say "damn all."

Silas scratched his ear. Same ravine that ran out past his folks' barn, he reckoned. Same one. But up this way it sounded foreign and strange. Everything seemed foreign and strange up this way. Even the root bark that looked like alligator skin. Just two miles from home, but everything seemed strange up here. Leave it to folks like this to live in a strange place. Still had an outhouse, though.

dow. Suppertime, Silas reckoned. He thought he smelled cornbread maybe. Last supper for that old man. Last supper. One shot at the bib of that old man's overalls. That's all it would take to make everything all right again. One shot.

Silas scratched his eyelid, then pulled at the gallouses of his overalls. Strange, the way you have to scratch when you're trying to be still. Strange how those roots looked like alligator skin.

The spring on the screen door screeched. A shape formed up on the back porch. Damn it. The moon wouldn't be up for two hours or so. Dark. But that's why Silas was crouched just by the door of the outhouse. Three yards at most. Couldn't miss seeing, couldn't miss shooting. Not here.

Silas twisted his head, pointing his ear toward the path, trying to pull a sound from the mush the water made.

Nothing. Nothing. A form loomed up.

Silas caught his breath and hugged the shotgun's stock up against his shoulder. Just like dove hunting, now. Just like dove hunting, Silas told himself.

His finger twisted off the trigger and his body convulsed. It wasn't the daddy. Wasn't even one of the brothers. It was the girl.

Silas rolled up like a possum. He wasn't about to shoot a girl in the family. Not even this family. Even they deserved better than that. Even after what they did.

The door of the outhouse swung open, banged shut on its weighted chain. Silas strained hard to hear over the creek. Suddenly, it was important to hear her water, her water falling into the pit. He couldn't. And that upset him nearly enough to take a good shot right into the outhouse. Just kill her there with her undies down. Good enough for one of them.

But Silas didn't. Silas wasn't those kind of folks.

He'd seen men, cousins and uncles even, shoot squirrels out of their nests. That wasn't hunting. No. That's not the way a man does things. You don't shoot something on the solid. You don't shoot nothing standing still. Eating. Making water. It ain't right. Even in a feud. There's right and there's wrong.

The door swung open, banged shut. She. She trailed back into the dark. She shouldn't be one of them, should she. Or one of anybody around here. The way she moved.

Way he heard it, she was going to graduate from the high school. No, it wasn't right to kill a thing like that. Not even if she'd run. Silas wasn't those kind of folks. Not like her folks.

Silas stared hard into the dark.

She reappeared faintly on the porch. Disappeared into the house again. She'd be sad soon. Just like Silas was sad. That made him sorry, a little.

Why did it have to be her daddy? Why did Silas have to kill anybody at all? Don't be an ignoramus, Silas told himself. That's just the way things is. For everybody. You do what you have to do. Not always the easiest way possible, either. Like shooting a squirrel's nest. But an easy way, sometimes, like waiting for a man by his outhouse. Cause every man has to go there sooner or later. And every man has to die sooner or later. And some men have to kill somebody or other. Somehow or other. No matter what they'd rather be doing.

Silas rubbed his trigger finger against the bark on the roots of the oak tree. Just like alligator skin, he thought. The roots had spread out and hung on like the washes in a plowed hillside after a heavy rain.

The spring on the screen door screeched.

Silas waited patiently in the dark.

Jack Crumpler   *Lake Conroe*

STRANGER DANGER

"There's a Chinaman standing out in the street," I said after I finished drinking the glass of water.

Mom's eyes widened, she stiffened and balled both hands into fists—things she always did when alarmed. "What's he doing?"

"Just standing out there."

"Where exactly?"

"The street," I said a tad too quickly, my impatience showing. "Sorta halfway 'tween our house and the Peppers'."

She unballed her fists and walked with slow, short steps toward the living room, the way most people move when they're trying to creep up on something. When she got to the front window, she lifted a single slat of the closed blinds with her right index finger, bent closer and peered outside. After a good look, she let the slat fall back into place.

"Sittin' down," she said. "Back to us. Can't rightly tell if it's a Chinaman or what."

"Wearing a blue shirt?"

"Yessy-yessy."

I took a peek through the blinds. "Same guy. Chinaman."

"We better go next door and tell Charlie." Mom's hands were balled into fists again.

"Why?"

"'Cause there's a Chinaman out there. Like I always say, always say, when you see a stranger, you could be in danger."

Mom sometimes repeated words or phrases when she was agitated.

"What can Uncle Charlie do?"

"He'll know what to do, to do."

I headed for the front door, but Mom, in a harsh, hushed tone, said we should go through the back yard so the stranger wouldn't see us. In short order, we'd barged through Uncle Charlie's back door, knocking as we entered.

Mom called out, "Charlie, it's us."

"Come in," Mom's only brother yelled. He met us in the little dining room. "What's brought you two over?"

Mom blurted, "Denison here...he saw a Chinaman, a Chinaman, standin' out in the street, only now I think he's sittin' on the curb between our house and the Peppers'."

A mix of humor and incredulity crawled across Charlie's lined face, weathered from years of working outdoors as a heavy equipment operator for the City of Abilene. "What?" He spat the word.

"Saw him with my own eyes," I said.

"Chinaman, you say?" The grin had taken over his face. "Ain't no Chinamans

89

'round here that I know of."

"Well, that's what Denison saw," Mom said. "A Chinaman standin' in the street, only now he's sittin' on the curb."

Charlie laughed. "Denison, you some kind of expert on Chinamans?"

"No, sir, but that's what he is."

"Well," Charlie drawled as he pulled his grease-stained khaki pants higher on his paunch, "let's go have ourselves a look-see at this here Chinaman."

At Mom's suggestion, we exited through the back door, then skulked around the side of Uncle Charlie's house, the side away from where I'd seen the Chinaman. Charlie led the way.

"Shhhhh," Mom admonished as we reached the front corner of the house.

Charlie turned to face us. "Weren't gonna say anything. Why you shushing me?"

"We need to be careful," she answered. "Like I always say, when you see a stranger, you could be in danger."

Charlie scrunched up his face, turned and peeked around the corner of the house, then took a couple of steps so he could see past the clump of nandinas. Mom was so close behind she bumped into him when he stopped.

"Gimme a little room here," Charlie barked, then bent forward slightly as he took another peek. He straightened. "Be danged. Do believe that is so a Chinaman."

Both Mom and I crept forward, she to see around Charlie, me to see around Mom. The Chinaman had been facing in our direction, looking down the street, but turned away.

"What do you suppose he's doing, doing?" Her hands were balled into fists again.

"Well," Charlie began and swiped his right hand across his mouth, "I'd say at this red-hot moment, he's lookin' one way and then t'other, sorta like he's watching for somebody. Waitin' for a ride maybe."

"We better call the law," Mom said and added, "the law."

Charlie turned to face her. "Why's that? Don't think there's no law against bein' a Chinaman. Or standin' out in the street. Leastwise I never heard of no such laws."

"Could'a just robbed somebody, somebody, and is waiting out there for the getaway driver," Mom whispered.

Charlie laughed. "Yeah, I'm sure that's the way robbers work, all right."

"He might be a vagrant," I said.

"Thought you said he's a Chinaman," Charlie answered.

"A vagrant is...," Mom began.

"Aw, I know what a vagrant is," Charlie shot back. "Just funnin' the boy, but you got a point. Still and all, we don't know if he's a vagrant. Not sure he's a Chinaman. Could be a Jap or one of them there Viet-whatevers."

"Maybe we could just go out there and ask him," I suggested.

"Mercy no, no, no," Mom retorted.

"Why not?"

"Yeah, why not?" Charlie said. "Hell's bells...."

"No need to be vulgar in front of Denison here," Mom snapped.

"He just might be lost or somethin'." Charlie ignored Mom's admonition. "Could just need a ride somewheres."

The three of us pulled back to the edge of the house when the Chinaman took his first step east—in our direction, although he stayed in the street and gave no indication he saw us. At the corner of Twelfth and Matador, he turned north and strode out of sight as we crept into the front yard then closer to the curb to prolong our view of him.

Charlie slapped the sides of his legs with both hands. "Well, vagrant Chinaman or no, he's a gone goslin' now."

"We still ought to call the law," Mom said. She had relaxed her fists.

"And say what?" Charlie giggled. "We thought you occifers should know that we ain't got a Chinaman standing out in our street anymore."

Mom took a quick, deep breath, the kind that made a hushed snort noise, the sound she usually made when she was vexed. "No good havin' people like that about."

"Mom says if you see a stranger, you're seeing danger." I grinned.

Mom scowled at me.

Uncle Charlie took an exaggerated look up and down the street. He pulled the plug of Day's Work tobacco from his shirt pocket, peeled back the wrapper, bit some off, returned the package to his pocket and shifted the chew into his left check. He turned toward us. "No Chinaman. Nobody whatsoever. No stranger. No danger. Believe I'll go in and have me a glass of iced tea. Hotter'n usual this spring. Want some?"

We joined Uncle Charlie for iced tea.

JG Butts   *Midland*

NIGHT GOLD

Like a rare fifty-dollar gold piece
wedged in the earth's folds,
the August moon creeps up
on an unguarded well site,
slips out to sit on the rim of
blackness, and throwing long, dark
shadows there and there and there,
it just hangs like a fiery spotlight,
a smoldering orange hole in the night,
watching the pump-jack, like a spy:

But, never looking up, never
acknowledging its nightly trespasser,
the black finger keeps pumping, up and
down, like a great iron bird perched
on the brim of the oil basin,
dipping and sipping, tilting and drinking,
and dipping and sipping
in perpetual motion,
schlep, schlup, schlep, schlup,
sucking crude from the payzone.

Slowly deflating, the fat moon sails away
in one giant arc, and like a grand
frosted opal, it lights up
another working night.

Irwin Wingo   *Weatherford*

CORPUS CHRISTI

Wilfred Ray woke up as the eastern horizon was just startin' to show a little spunk of pink. He felt tolerable well except for a small, dull ache in his side. He knew that he ought to be afflicted with a horse killin' hangover- he had drunk a shot of Jack Daniels the night before and had chased the taste of it out of his mouth with Lone Star beer- twenty-one of 'em. Still had three full cans left of the case he had promised to take back to Fuzzy and the boys at the ranch.

It was cramped in the front of the old pick-up. The cab was crowded with spent beer cans, the empty box they had come in, a sack of pinto beans, a couple of cans of coffee, a smushed up and leakin' box of Ritz Crackers, two tins of Skoal smokeless, and some bags of Redman chewin' tobacco. All these sundries were scattered here and there along with his hat, his boots, his socks, his jeans, and his shirt: Wilfred Ray was as nekkid as any day old jaybird.

He reached out the window for the outside door handle- the inside one was busted.- so he could purchase for himself a little bit of elbow room. He noticed his hand was stiff. With a major effort he balled it into a fist. It didn't hurt him none, it just had about the same spryness as an old fence post. He brought his other hand across his body in order to rub the offendin' one and found that it was stiff too. With his left fingers he could feel something was wrong with the back of his right hand. It felt like he had a hole in it.

Wilfred Ray shot up in the seat and pulled his hand in front of his face. The light was still weak but he could make out that he did for sure have him a hole in his hand all right. He looked harder and saw he had a hole in the other as well. He had holes a little bigger than a nickel which went all the way through and came out his palms.

He managed to open the door up and step down to the ground. But his feet, it turned out, were stiffer than his hands and he fell to the desert dirt with a whop. He lay there a second, then sat up. He was lucky, he figgered, that he hadn't went face first into a Prickly Pear. Wilfred Ray looked at his feet. They, too, had been pierced, but like his hands they didn't pain him any. In a minute he was able to loosen them up enough so that he could stand upright. He hobbled to the back of the pick up.

As he sat on the open and bunged-up tail-gate of the truck's beat-up bed, his attention turned to the little throb in his side. He twisted his head down and saw he had an ugly cut there, just below his ribs. He eased his still stubborn movin' thumb into the gash. The slit was deep, much too bad of a wound not to hurt any more than it did. Wilfred Ray was plumb stumped that he wasn't bleedin' like a stuck hog. He figgered he had done gone the night before and pissed off somebody but good.

Wilfred Ray made his way back to the cab and slipped into his clothes. The stiffness in his hands and feet had mostly let up with the stretchin' he had done. He crawled behind the wheel. The truck's starter caught on the third or fourth try and the engine coughed itself to life with a belch of gray smoke. He was back on the road headin' off in the direction of the ranch.

About six miles down the highway, just as he passed Contrabando Creek, Wilfred Ray saw Miguel's old Diamond T flatbed in the right-hand bar ditch. There were about thirty wetbacks millin' around the faded-out truck that rightly ought to have been in a museum. Miguel, when not busy fathering children with his three wives, two over the border and one in Presidio, hauled illegals across the river. He stood up from where he was bent over a rear tire and waved Wilfred Ray down.

Wilfred Ray pulled over.

"Got ya some tire trouble?"

"Some," said Miguel. "Got it fixed though. Took a while 'cause one of the lug nuts had the edges buggered up pretty bad. But why it was I stopped you was that I got me a little leak in my fuel line and I'm 'bout out of gas. I gotta get this load of 'backs part ways up to Marfa on the old road. I'll get paid when I get them there. You have any extra gas on you?"

Wilfred Ray pointed towards a couple of dented-up, five-gallon jerry cans on the back of his truck.

"Go on ahead and help yourself to it."

He knew Fuzzy would go and get out of joint when he got back to the ranch without, not only the beer, but the gas as well but it was the law of the road in this place of long spaces and few people. You took care of folks in need and they took care of you. Besides it was for Miguel. He was good for it: he had helped the boys on the ranch more than a few times. Fuzzy would have done the same thing.

As Wilfred Ray watched Miguel pour the gas into his truck he also looked around at Miguel's passengers. It never ceased to cause him wonder to how many of these folks could get into and onto a single vehicle. He looked hard at the wetbacks all round him. This was, he figgered, a pretty pitiful crew.

He said as much to Miguel.

"They've had it hard all right, " Miguel agreed. "Real green sorts from down south of Mexico City. Had trouble all the way and those bastards who got 'em to the river didn't feed 'em for two days. I ain't aiming' on doin' business with those hombres again. If I had known how it was goin' to be I'd have butchered up a goat to feed 'em. All the food I got is what Rosa packed for me- five sorry little tortillas and a couple of pieces cabrito about the size of my finger."

Wilfred Ray felt strange. Like he had never felt before.

"Let me have that food," he said.

"Sure, uh, OK," answered Miguel as he looked at Wilfred Ray in a surprised way. " Just don't eat in front of 'em here. The little kids are awful hungry."

Wilfred Ray took the meat and thin tortillas.

"Here senora," he said as he approached a middle-aged woman. He gave her some food and moved on to the next person and then the next.

"Here Nina. Here Senor. Here Madre," he intoned in a soft voice as he passed the food around. Everyone had some and he started over again, then again, then again. Finally, everybody was full. There were smiles on the brown faces and love was bustin' from their hearts like leaves bustin' out on a Cottonwood tree in the springtime.

Wilfred Ray had the leftover food collected up. There were two tow sacks stuffed plumb full of tortillas and he had to dump icy water out of the forty-four quart cooler on the back of the pick-up for the leftover meat. The cooler just barely held all of it. There were nine dozen frosted cookies come from somewhere for the kids. These folks could eat well until they got to Ft. Worth where they would mow the lawns, shingle the roofs and keep the houses of the rich people there.

Wilfred Ray pushed himself on through the throng of appreciatin' and adorin' folks as they gently tried to lay their hands on him and implored him in their native tongue to bless them. He was more than a mite scared and was red-faced embarrassed something awful.

He got into the old Dodge pick-up and sped off down the road. He looked at his hands on the steerin' wheel. The holes were gone. He knew without looking that his feet and side were all healed up as well.

Wilfred Ray looked at the dry, red colored mountains all about him. He knew Fuzzy would be pissed about the gas, the beer and the loss of the cooler. But Fuzzy would get over it.

Patrick Bennett   *Abilene*

DIFFICULTIES OF THE MODERN

I'm wanting to learn to write a sonnet
But, Lovey, they want me to learn a new
Damned computer program, instead. I chew
My nails, thumb through the manual on it
In digital Greek, study the Monet
Hanging over my desk, grass green, sky blue,
Belle beautiful. A trifle hazy true,
But nearer the place a wight might write a sonnet.

I want to start by picking out my rhymes
But first I must pick the proper icon;
I grind my teeth and curse these evil times,
Paths too rocky to peddle my bike on;
I want to work on meter, dance on dimes,
Instead must squeeze a dumb mouse I dump dislike on.

Mary Ann Taylor   *Dallas*

SHIBBOLETH

Mexia: Not Meksia, not Maheea, Bexar: not Beksar
For that matter, Sa' nAngelo not San Angelo

Corsicana is such a name. The scan is trochee, sure enough,
But a lyric, an inflection that is more than spelling.
Corsicana (you have to know how) Corsicana like
Refugio Kountze Kerens

I was stuck in the mud, once, in Corsicana.
When I called the relentless 800 number,
I was spoken to rudely, imagine, although
It was unwise to make light of it all Anahuac
Leakey DeSoto Terrell

I spoke nicely to the woman at the Exxon counter.
Need help? She asked.
No, triple A will come, someday.
She called Jack: Got anybody who could come out on the triple A?
Call comin' in now? Okay, she's right here. Car's down a little ways.
He'll be on out, ma'am.
I see they have manners in Corsicana
Groesbeck Cuero

Other travelers, all less foolish than I, came in and bought
And visited the back room and left again.
Although nimble, Jack was not so quick.
Manchaca Elgin Lancaster

I sat longer than any stayed, until it grew dark.
So Flossie (of course, she could never move to Dallas with such a name)
And I got acquainted: She wondered, Got business out here?
Yes, a bit. I'm fixin' to go see some folks over on Route 2.
I come to Corsicana ever so often.
(Don't usually talk like this though).
Waxahachie Montague Sachse

She nodded wisely in her country way, though worldly worn by the interstate.
To her dog Buster: Let's go turn on them lights while nobody's here.

Again, as if a hex with her wrong-specied familiar, sprinkling her cant over me,
Walking, smiling, chanting: Let's go turn on them lights while nobody's here.

And I sat and was Nobody, astonished and glad to be among them,
Among those who knew me and not Somebody here, can't go out
Can't turn on them lights now
But nobody is so we can.
It is a sweet key to know, to say:
Italy Bronte Buda
Let's go turn on them lights while
Nobody's here
Corsicana Corsicana I know how Corsicana
While nobody's here.

Larry D. Thomas   *Houston*

AUNT MAE AND UNCLE BOB'S ROCKER

For the last ten years of his life,
in rain or shine, he shuffled
to his rocker on the porch
to while away his hours.

It sits in the same place
it sat when he died a decade back.
Its presence comforts her:
the way the slats of its seat

slightly sag as if still laden
with his weight; the way at night,
when the wind's just right,
a floorboard creaks with its rocking.

She's left it there to play out
its usefulness, to play with the sun,
in the tournament of dust,
the checkers of light and shadow.

Ruth Hudson Savage   *Arlington*

VIRTUAL WEDLOCK

I sit at my breakfast table
in my sunroom on a lazy Saturday,
visualizing Harry and the breakfast
we should be sharing.
He always liked oatmeal
with brown sugar and lots of butter,
a whole-wheat muffin and coffee,
dark and steaming.
I always had my boiled egg,
a slice of dry toast, and orange juice.
There wasn't much need for
conversation and the birds and
squirrels furnished entertainment.
Harry read the stock-market news
to me if he did well,
if not, he just said — "humph!"
I read *Dear Abby* to him, especially
if I thought it was advice he needed;
it was more effective if it didn't
come directly from me.
I visualize Harry's blue eyes
peeking over his glasses
just above the headline of
The Austin American Statesman.
He would mutter, "would you...",
push his cup toward the carafe
and I would.
I would ask, "are you going to..."
and he would say "already did".
Verbal shorthand, I called it.
Came in handy when mind-reading
wasn't enough, which it usually was.
So it is with old companions.
Shared experiences merge in the
mist of time, the edges of an
individual blur, like the corms of a
canna; you just grow together.
Then, with the cut of the pruner's
shear, one is taken, the other left
tied in knots that blind.

In the Field:
Photographs of Texas Flowers

William J. Scheick

Flowers appear on the earth ...
the singing of birds is come.
Canticles 2:12

Surprise, I imagine, keeps me on the look-out—the surprise of a dollop of wild-flower color in an otherwise unappealing overcast hollow or sun-swept field. In the play of light and shadow some Texas flowers are flagrant; others modest, even retiring. Some require a simple glance; others insist on close company. But always there is a beauty that mysteriously surpasses floral function. Flowers bless the eye.

What the eye easily receives strangely resists my camera lens. Transient beauty exerts its own design. It is not still life. Sturdy orange trumpets tremble in the breeze, fragile red columbines incline gravely earthward, loud yellowbells huddle tightly against the wind, soft lavender bindweed blooms streak through shadows, and creamy Spanish daggers stab blindingly into stark skies. No flower poses.

Behind the camera I sympathize with Maerten van Heemskerck behind his canvas of "Saint Luke Painting the Virgin." From what angle is a polymorphous wonder to be rendered? Emphasize but one feature in the miraculous texture? Surrender to a simultaneous welter of perspectives? And in either instance, how close can artists come in representing what has so riveted their attention?

Even when I kneel to steady the zoom lens, none of my photographs come close to their green-fused subjects. So I simply welcome each day's wild-flower perspective and always await tomorrow's renewed surprises in the field.

Leslie Williams   *Midland*

EVENSONG

"Don't forget me," Beulah Potts called up to the bus driver. "I'm too tired to pull the string."

This morning her husband, Mr. Billy Potts, had sat there on the edge of the bed, his old white face mealy, stubbly; just sat there picking at the hair on his paunch, watching some gun show on the T.V. Beulah had said, "Well, at least at the Fairs' they have air conditioning and Mr. Fair don't keep beer cans all over the living room, like some people I could mention."

Mr. Billy Potts just sat on the bed, scratching at the gray hairs in his belly button.

"I'm so tired I could die," said Beulah, gathering up her bag, getting ready to leave.

Her husband called out from the bedroom, "You just give me one good reason why you keep going over there."

She had closed the door without answering.

Beulah looked out the bus window. The problem was, she didn't know why she kept going over there, day after day. It wasn't the money. Mr. Billy Potts had kept his job at the Performance Automotive for eleven straight months.

It sure wasn't the hours why she kept coming. By the time she got off the food line at Luby's Cafeteria and caught the bus over here, she was already beat. And she still had hours to go before she got home.

"Here you go, Beulah," said the driver, as the bus stopped at the corner of Pecos and Cherry Lane.

"Thanks, Cecil." She stood up. Maybe she kept coming for the little one, though Lord knows whether he noticed or not.

"Look nice today," said Cecil, as Beulah lugged off her shopping bag filled with crossword puzzles, crackers, a bouquet of plastic flowers, and her blue scarf.

"Oh, Cecil," she blushed. "You sure know how to make an old girl feel good." Count on Cecil to notice her new wig. If she did say so herself, this brown wig was elegant.

Seven months ago, she answered the ad in the paper for a night sitter, and she'd been coming over here ever since. This part of Austin, especially since all the flowers had come out, looked like the Garden of Eden, if Eve had never of eaten the apple, and if she and Adam had settled down and had a family.

But it wasn't any paradise here, no sir. Not at the Fair's house. Not with their little one dying and all.

If Beulah had a rich Daddy instead of a circuit preacher who left all five of them when Beulah was six, she'd have wanted to grow up in a house like the Fairs'. It had two stories, yellow bricks, and pillars; and inside it had wall-to-wall carpet in every room, with drapes to match. In fact, Beulah would like to live in the Fair's house just for one week, all by herself. But she wasn't starving, so she couldn't complain.

And it wasn't the things of this world that mattered anyway.

She knocked on the door. The Fairs had a big gold lion on their doorknocker. It was beautiful.

"Thank God you are finally here. I wish you had a car instead of that *unreliable bus*." Mrs. Fair was fidgety, as usual.

"Yes, Ma'am," said Beulah. She didn't say so, but she also wished she had a car.

Mrs. Fair looked fit to kill. She was built like one of those fashion models, blonde and skinny, and tonight she had on a slinky black dress and lots of diamonds.

"Martha had to leave early, and I've been stuck trying to get ready for the symphony and keep my eye on Wallace. God--" she bent over and hitched up the strap of her high heel--"I would just die if something happened to him and I was the only one here."

"Yes, ma'am." Beulah walked across the room and put her shopping bag in the corner.

"Mr. Fair's at the office, of course. He'll wait until the last moment possible, you'll see--then he'll tear himself away, swing by here, and pick me up. Sometimes, Mrs. Potts, I wonder if it's occurred to him that I might be here alone, by myself, when Wally dies."

Personally, Beulah thought Mr. Fair cared about a lot of things, more than Mrs. Fair. He was just too hurt to show it. Lots of nights right before the cab arrived, Mr. Fair came into Wallace's room, and sat watching Wally breathe; sat there in his fancy velvet robe, looking at his little baby.

When he'd hear Beulah getting ready to tiptoe on out, Mr. Fair would say from the shadows where he was sitting, "Be careful. Don't get wet out there, " or "Looks like we're going to have some pretty weather coming up."

Once she thought she'd heard him say, "Why?" She stood there at the door, not knowing how to respond. She didn't know if he meant, "Why did Wallace have the growth in the first place?" or "Why didn't the good Lord take him away and not drag out his dying like this?" Or maybe he didn't say "Why?" at all; maybe he just sighed.

She had finally said, "Good night, Mr. Fair. I'm awful sorry." She wanted to say something else. Something that would make him feel better. Instead she walked out into the night rain, forgetting her umbrella.

"Beulah," Mrs. Fair was saying, "run on back and check on Wally while I change purses. This brown one won't do at all."

"Yes, ma'am." Beulah heard her fumbling around, clanking her lipstick and comb.

Mrs. Fair called out, "There's a left-over pork chop in the refrigerator if you get hungry." Mrs. Fair was nervous, like she walked on hot coals. But she was always that way. The doctor said it was her metabolism.

Wally's room looked like a carnival. They'd hung all kind of colored animals and clowns from the ceiling over his crib, and when the wind blew through the window, all the toys went crazy and the strings got tangled up.

Wally never noticed. No, he just lay the same way, day in, day out, his little gray eyes staring into space. Beulah bent over the crib, tucking in his blanket. Mrs. Fair came and stood next to her, and they both looked at Wally's drooping face and the growth on the side of his head, big as a cabbage.

The first time Beulah saw Wally, she almost gagged at the growth stuck there, like the head of a furry Siamese twin.

Mrs. Fair flung herself into the armchair across the room. "God, Mrs. Potts, what did I ever do wrong? All my friends have such beautiful children." She pushed back her hair with her hand. "Well, anyway, I'm glad I can't have any more. Glad."

She appeared again at the side of the crib. She leaned over and touched Wally's gray, sunken cheek, whispering, "Oh, little one."

Then she turned abruptly to Beulah and said, "I have something for you." Beulah waited by the side of the crib while Mrs. Fair left the room. She was only gone a minute before she came back in carrying a sky blue silk kimona.

"Here," she said. "I bought it on a binge, and it isn't my color. I know it will fit you, here," and she held it up, draping it over Beulah's shoulders. Beulah stared at the fabric. It had flying birds stitched in matching sky blue thread.

"It's the most beautiful thing I ever seen," said Beulah, running her coarse hands over the silk. It was so beautiful Mr. Billy Potts would probably think she stole it.

Mrs. Fair bit at the corner of her nail. "I don't know what I'd do if you ever stopped coming."

Just then the front door opened and Mrs. Fair dashed out of the room. Beulah, still standing with the kimona draped over her shoulders, heard her say, "Wouldn't want you to lose a single billable hour."

"I'm sorry, Ellen."

"Don't touch me, please. We'll be late."

Mr. Fair sighed. "Is Mrs. Potts here yet?" Mr. Fair started walking down the hall, and Beulah had folded the kimona and set it on a chair before he appeared at the door of Wally's room. He was a big man, steady, and like the son Beulah wished she had. Someone you could lean on.

"Hello, Mrs. Potts. How are you?"

"Oh, fine. You?"

Mrs. Fair yelled down the hall, "I'll be waiting in the car." She slammed the front door.

"We'll be at the symphony. The number's on the bulletin board if you need to reach us." He added, "You look nice today. I like your . . ." he hesitated, "hair."

Beulah blushed. "Oh, Mr. Fair. It's my new wig."

"Well, it looks good. Call us if you need us."

"You have a nice evening. Don't you worry about nothing, you hear?"

After they left, the evening closed in on Beulah and Wally in the small room. She put on the kimona over her clothes and looked at herself for a minute in the mirror. She felt bad for thinking Mrs. Fair didn't care about Wally.

She changed Wally's diaper, then sat down in the rocking chair next to him, listening to the cicadas and watching the clowns twirl above his bed. After awhile, she got up and brought the cold pork chop back. She turned off all the lights except a lamp in the corner, and she licked the pork chop clean, going at it slowly to make it last as long as possible.

Wally moved. Beulah got up to check on him. One tiny foot stuck out from the blanket. She leaned down and covered it. As she straightened up, her wig got entangled with one of the clown mobiles. It took her some time to free herself from a cluster of balloons. She was glad Mr. Fair wasn't watching her.

Wally started to cry. Beulah leaned over and lifted him carefully out of his crib. She wrapped his blanket around him and sat down in the rocking chair. He was a dead-weight, like a two-headed sack of oats. Most little ones at this age were walking around, getting into trouble every time you turned your back. Wally was nearly one-and-a-half, and he couldn't even hold his head up. He smelled nice, like baby powder--there wasn't the smell of death about him--and his skin was soft, like any other baby's. Wally hiccupped.

Beulah looked down at him. One of his ears was a cute little ear, but the other was deformed. It did make you wonder about the way of things.

Beulah didn't care if he was shuddersome to look at. He was one of God's creatures, and he was still alive. She figured she had an obligation to give him what comfort she could, so she rocked him in the rocking chair.

Though she didn't sing too well, she started in on "Swing Low, Sweet Chariot." She figured it wouldn't matter to Wally what it sounded like. Besides, it gave her some comfort to think of a big gold chair coming to take Wally and her both to a place with lots of light, a place where people's bones didn't hurt anymore from tiredness.

William W. Woods   *Kerrville*

TO THE YOUNG MAN WHO WILL COMFORT MY DAUGHTER SEVENTEEN YEARS FROM NOW

look, I know you're out there already
and with a father's fierce passion and love
I can't help but dislike you a little already
for someday taking her away

because this morning at 4am
when she stood up in her crib
and called out to me
awakened by some terrible nightfears

and I stumbled down the darkened hallway
scooped her up in my arms
held her close and tight, calmed her
we went to the sofa: she fell back

to that heavy deep baby sleep,
but as she did clinging to my shirt
she said over and over again:
"good daddy, good daddy"

and in that moment I sensed you
were out there, waiting
soon she will cry against
your chest, needing your support

listen: it might seem like something silly to you
a failing grade on a midterm exam
an argument with a best friend
but for god's sake act like you care

hold her head gently brush back her hair
press against her closely but
this is not the time for your romantic advances
please, I'm begging you, comfort her well

when I can't be there

Sherry Craven   *Canyon*

MARRIED THREE TIMES

My mother says, holding coffee and reign in
equal authority, that Mary Sue Martindale
has been married four times. We receive that this
as she intends—like news of heart trouble, or bankruptcy.

The air is hushed like the waiting room in a doctor's office;
mindless sullenness fills the carefully appointed living room,
and I am careful not to spill droplets of myself or my coffee
on the velvet blue sofa. We become sentries guarding the
gates to self-respect.

Mary Sue is small and sexy and has
long over-processed hair that
in spite of ourselves, we all envy,
the way she slithers up to our husbands and they like it.
The way her bellybutton marks a spot we are uneasy about.
The way we feel virtuous yet unfulfilled, cheated.

I wait, having been married three times myself,
like a cocker spaniel, waiting for its master,
to find the tin with the doggie treats,
raised on my haunches of hope,
eager, anxious, hopeful for a reprieve,
sanctified sanction of my own actions.

Like the priest, my mother
hands me a wafer of generosity
returning my own body to me:
"But," she says, "you did it all so nicely."

I ride the breath of relief
exhaled from my friends' hearts
over their matching coffee cups,
and float back to myself,

like at the communion rail when I
know the wafer is not really Jesus,
but I accept the blessing
with bowed head anyway.

Tony Zurlo & Vivian Lu   *Fort Worth*

A SIMPLE CONVERSATION

I talk to you everyday—
a simple conversation
about roses and gardens
dandelions in grass

should we plant wild flowers
on the hill? run ivy up the stairs?
how to protect our China Doll
from winter's freeze?

a few words each day
flung into turbulent air
casual thoughts expressed
by nature's breath

I hold up half the sky
while waiting into the nighttime
of our lives, apart—
endless oceans apart

I marvel at our lives
and wonder about eternity
and supporting half of heaven—
will there be time for simple talk?

SPEECHLESS RESPONSE

The voice of your simple conversation
travels faster than light
Just in a second
it echoes in my mind

My answer is the tears of two rivers—
the Yellow River and the Yangzi River
with a silent sound of singing water
'Cause I am speechless in response

Susan Marie Lewis   *Brownwood*

ALONE AT FORTY-EIGHT

This widowhood is like real estate.
Seems yesterday I went for a premium,
had curb appeal and the latest gadgets,
looked good. Now it's time to fix up
and paint my way back on the market.
I probably need new wiring.
The rest of the neighborhood has gone rental
and light commercial. I do have a solid
foundation, brick veneer, roof doesn't leak,
and the mortgage is definitely paid.

Mada Plummer   *Pflugerville*

BENNEDENE

before the sun
arrived, just about the time
a deep blue october sky
was turning over,
i came back
with a flashlight
to search
for the fresh footprints
i left in your flowerbed
the evening before.
they got erased
by torrential night rains,
and slashing wet winds
that cleaned the air, silenced
the streets, and fiercely shook
the small elms
in your front yard
until they dangled,
as if unplugged.
"the will of God
will not take us
where
the grace of God
cannot
keep us."
in sisterly harmony,
we still share giggles,
swap recipes
for a happy day,
plan a sunday afternoon
tea time and swing
back and forth until sunset.
the first time
i crossed the threshold
of the "pink house"
on east 13th street,
familiar spirits
met me at the front door,
tore my breast, split my blood.

from my great grandmother's
indigo scarf, to my father's coffee cup
stain on your kitchen table, and
my mother's apron on the doorknob,
my sister's framed smile on the mantle.
the sound of your quiet
footsteps across hardwood floors
rivals slow, deep sleep heartbeats;
the sight of the old piano
in the corner stands
like forgotten cobweb;
the lacey curtains that hang
at the windows reminded me of
how my mother waited, watched
listened for us to come home
in playground dirty uniforms.
before the sun
goes away today,
we should
walk deliberately
in the garden
among the tall grass,
leave behind our
footprints.

Patricia M. Murphy   *Witchita Falls*

SHELTER

The Macintoshes are going down
into their bomb shelter
To play Chinese checkers.
Mitzi, the cocker spaniel, stays with neighbors
Tammy brings along Nancy Drew
Tucker has G.I. Joe and a crew cut
Life Magazine is there with
Blinding Leicas to tell the story
Of how to save yourself.

Nothing deters those Macintoshes
Not Mabel's grandfather's funeral
Not the closeout sale at Steinman's Dry goods
Tiny gives up Thursday night bingo
After three months they crawl out.

That bomb shelter cost a lot of money
Tiny Macintosh couldn't meet
The mortgage
Mabel drank away the *Life* royalties
Sitting in Tucker's college fund
He had to drop out of Bowling Green
A mortar vaporized him at Khe Sanh
Tammy does crack

Some say it was the three months
Packed like Norway sardines
That caused the fallout
But it was the waiting that did it
Crowded into a Levittown bungalow
For twenty years, walled in
By hand-me-down dreams
Going in when they were told

When they finally stumbled out
Weak, exhausted, starving
They must have wondered
Why Wantagh was still standing
And Wal-Mart had outlived
Edward Teller.

Karen Bingham Pape   *Midland*

COYOTE NIGHT

In the oil field a giant hand
pistons up and down
upanddown upanddown
pumping
oil from the grease-soaked
desert ground.

The pumpjack's
metronomic sound
magnifies to grinding groan
echoes the coyote's cry
in the moonlit night
the call of a woman in her lover's arms
in a motel on Highway 80
where dreams die hard north
of interstate, flat countryside
where trucks brake
and turn only when they have
no other place to hide.

Joy Wright   *Denton*

MIRAGES

Lily and her friend Roberta stood at the rear of the church sanctuary and surveyed the people seated in the mahogany pews. Although available seating remained throughout the sanctuary, a respectable crowd was already on hand with thirty minutes to go before the special music program began. A revivalistic songfest wasn't exactly Lily's idea of a fun-filled evening, but she wanted to please Roberta and so had agreed to come.

"What a pretty little church," Lily commented as she noted the kaleidoscope of color in the stained glass windows and the aisles carpeted in bright blue. Even the mahogany pews sported soft velvet cushions in matching blue. *Ah, ha! Comfortable Christianity,* she thought. *At least I won't go home with a tired butt tonight.* She was glad Roberta couldn't read her mind. She didn't want to irritate her friend who attended church there, and, after all, what was wrong with being comfortable AND Christian?

Roberta nodded her head, and the daisies on her straw hat bobbed happily up and down as if they too agreed. "Yes, the church IS pretty," she agreed. "We've worked very hard to make it a pleasant place to worship."

Lily was growing tired of standing. She brushed back a strand of graying hair from her face and took a deep breath. "Well, Roberta, I need to sit down. Where shall we sit? We could have the entire front row to ourselves, and everybody would know we're here. Wouldn't you like that?"

"Forget it, Lily." Roberta shook her head.

"Aw, nobody ever sits on the front pew. But I'll do it next time I go to my own church. That'll be my big rebellion against tradition," Lily said wryly.

Roberta grinned. "The front row's too far for you to walk anyway. Let's sit about halfway."

Lily glared at Roberta. "I believe I could summon the strength to get to the front. Nevertheless, we'll sit where you prefer. Just lead the way." Down the center aisle they went, Roberta leading the way in her happy hat, flowered dress, and lace-up boots, Lily following in her black silk slacks, zebra blouse, and silver shoes.

About halfway to the front, Roberta stopped and slid into a pew on the right, Lily right on her tail. They sat down, and almost immediately Lily froze on the edge of the seat, her gaze focused on something slightly to her right, her hands grasping the pew in front of her, her mouth open to blow out some breath. Roberta heard her gasp and looked over at her. She reached out to touch Lily gently on the arm, but before she could say anything, Lily began hissing like a tire losing air. "Not here! We can't sit here! Anywhere but here!"

"What's the matter, dear?" Roberta asked, noticing that people were staring at them, especially a smiling, attractive, older man in the next pew. But Lily was already on her feet and scurrying down the row. This time, Roberta followed her across the sanctuary where they plopped down in an empty pew.

Lily was panting; her breasts were heaving. "For God's sake...," she hissed.

"What in the world's the matter with you?" asked Roberta.

"Just a minute...I'll tell you in a minute," Lily gasped out between breaths. Finally she was able to explain. "You sat down right behind my ex-husband; that's Travis down there. I think he's with his cousin Carl."

Roberta laughed. "Of all places for me to pick."

"I don't want him to think I sat down behind him on purpose!"

"Heaven forbid," said Roberta. She rolled her eyes, then looked back to where they had been. "Which one is he?" she asked, leaning forward and craning her neck like a turkey gobbler's.

"He's the man two seats from the end, next to the hoary-headed fellow with the beard."

"Oh, I see. Your ex is the cute one."

Lily's eyebrows rushed together in a frown. "Not so cute if you have to live with him. He drank, you know." She paused, then added, "I wonder where Travis's wife is. And I wonder what he's doing in church. He NEVER went to church the whole seven years WE were married."

Roberta was still staring across the sanctuary. She chuckled softly. "Well, Lily, maybe you'll find out. Here he comes."

"Oh, Lord." Lily straightened her shoulders, smoothed back her flyaway hair, lifted her chin, and watched Travis walk quickly, a youthful spring in his step, up the outside aisle and down the center aisle until he stopped alongside the pew where they sat.

He smiled, brown eyes dancing behind bifocals, and gestured towards the vacant space next to Lily. Then he leaned forward in what was almost a bow. "Mind if I sit down here for a few minutes?"

Lily looked up at him and smiled back, all annoyance and apprehension gone. *No need for me to be tacky,* she thought. *After all, we buried the hatchet years ago because of April; she's the only thing we ever did right.* "Not at all," she said. "Please do sit down." He followed her bidding.

They had not seen each other in thirteen years.

It seemed inconceivable to Lily that she had ever been married to this man. They hadn't "gone together" then and they didn't "go together" now. Even so, as she looked up into his face, she felt a familiar tug, an attraction that time and sorrow and rage had not obliterated. To Lily, Travis looked much the same except for the thinning gray hair. His face, although no longer the "baby face" of his youth, remained relatively unlined, and his body was lean and firm.

"How are you?" They both spoke at once.

Then Lily smiled at him and said, "You go first."

"Oh, I'm doing fine," he said. "And how about you?" He leaned down so close that their faces were almost touching.

"I'm all right," she answered. Then she introduced Roberta to him, and they greeted each other, murmured the usual "pleased to meet you(s)", and shook hands.

"You're looking good, Lily," he said, as he studied her face. "You're pretty. You're still pretty. You always were."

"Why, thank you. You're looking well too." She turned her head away from him and looked around the sanctuary. "Where's your wife?"

"Oh, Clorinda's not feeling good. She picked up a spring cold and decided to stay home tonight."

"I see," Lily said, relieved that no one was likely to beat her over the head with a hymnal, not that Clorinda had ever been known for violence. Then, motioning towards the other side of the sanctuary, she asked, "Is that Cousin Carl over there? The one with all the hair?"

"Yeah, that's Carl."

"Well, I thought it was but I couldn't be sure. I'll bet it's been twenty years since we've seen each other. I never would've thought he'd have so much hair in his old age."

"You want to go say 'hello'?" Travis reached for her arm.

But Lily shook her head. "No, I think not. I'll just stay where I am." Lily had long since stopped rushing to greet people she hadn't seen in years. Either they didn't know who she was (even though she always gave her name) or their response was less than enthusiastic. Some even looked at her as if to say, "What in hell are you so pleased about?" After several such experiences, she decided to bide her time and let others come to her. Some, like Cousin Carl, stared steadfastly in other directions, sometimes scrutinizing entire rooms but never letting their gaze fall on her. Others, however, were as delighted as if they'd run across Miss America. Like Travis, for instance. Now HE was delighted!

Lily turned back to face him. "What are you doing here anyway?" It seemed very strange to her that they were sitting side by side in a church sanctuary. Pity that they hadn't tried it years ago.

"I came to spend the weekend with Carl. His girl Carrie Lou's leading the singing tonight, and we're all going fishing tomorrow."

"Speaking of singing," said Lily, "it looks to me as if they're getting ready to start. You'd better get back to your own seat before old Carl gets the wrong idea about what we're doing."

"Aw, I don't care what he thinks." Travis leaned forward. He stood up and looked down at her. "I'll be back during intermission."

And, indeed, he did come back when the singing stopped—when they'd run down the roster of hymns such as "Shall We Gather at the River?" "Onward, Christian Soldiers!" "Bringing in the Sheaves," "There Is a Fountain Filled With Blood," "In the Garden," and "The Old Rugged Cross". Of course, he and Lily had sneaked peeks at each other throughout the singing, especially when the congregation tore into "He's the Lily of the Valley, the Bright and Morning Star, He's the fairest of ten thousand to my soul". Then he came back and sat down beside her on the cushioned pew, and she felt the easy pressure of his body against hers, and somehow it felt right.

"We have about a fifteen minute break, Lily," Travis said. "There's still so much to say. I want to know how you really are. April said you'd quit smoking."

"Yes, I did." She looked away from him.

"Lung damage?" he asked.

"Yes." She nodded.

"I'm sorry." Travis reached out and touched her arm.

Lily smiled. "Oh, I'm all right. The damage is minor."

"I haven't managed to quit smoking yet," he said.

"I know. I can smell it," she answered. "But you did quit drinking. You're still going to AA, aren't you?"

"Oh, yeah, I have to do that."

"It's been about five years now, hasn't it?"

He smiled. "Six years, two months, and ten days."

"Good for you."

April had told her about the ordeal, had relayed information that Travis's wife Clorinda had given her since he never ventured near April when he'd been drinking. All secondhand information, and thank God for it. No more firsthand knowledge of his binges. So it was that Lily heard about but didn't see his sprees that lasted weeks, his near death from alcohol poisoning, his physical and mental problems, his hard work and money disappearing in an alcoholic haze, the months in the hospital, and the slow climb back. She'd seen enough during the seven years of their marriage. She'd wanted out early-on but for a long time had felt trapped, and she'd hoped beyond hope that he'd stop. It hadn't happened, of course. And now she was glad she'd divorced him and remarried and reared April, and had had a decent life, although James, her husband of thirty years, had died four years ago and she missed him. But she could never have lived in that god-awful mess with Travis like Clorinda had done for so many years.

Now Travis looked at her with his heart in his face. "I'm sorry," he said. "It was all my fault. I mean what happened between us, the divorce and all. I was dumb. I was stupid. Anybody can be dumb, but I was the worst." And he brought his fist down against his own leg. "Just look at you. You're pretty and good. What a fool, what a moron I was."

On and on he went with his apology until Lily grew irritated. After all, who left whom? "Travis," she said, "you have exactly the woman you need. Clorinda's stood beside you through some of the worst times in your life. She's been there for you in a way I'd never have been."

Travis snorted. "Clorinda probably just didn't have any place else she could go."

"Don't count on it," Lily said.

"You say that because you're so independent. You always were."

"I didn't want to be, Travis. I didn't have much choice."

"I know," he said. "It really was all my fault."

Lily smiled sweetly up at him; when she spoke, her voice literally oozed honeyed sincerity and remorse. "Now, now, Travis, don't be so hard on your-self," she soothed. "The blame for our breakup was never entirely yours. After all, I did lots of things you never found out about."

Travis's mouth fell open, and his eyes widened in shock. Lily thought it was priceless. She'd remember that look until the day she died. And she knew as sure as she lived that he'd wonder what the devil she'd done and he'd decide that she'd caroused around, and then he'd wonder how many and with whom. Maybe he wouldn't think about it much or for long, but he'd think about it some, yes indeedy. Lily stifled her giggles. Travis recovered quickly, though; she'd give him that. "No one could blame you, Lily, for anything you did," he said humbly.

After the intermission, Lily watched Travis return to his seat beside Cousin Carl. *This may be the last time I ever see him,* she thought. She turned to Roberta. "Did you hear very much of that conversation?"

"Enough to want to know more," Roberta answered.

"I'll tell you on the way home," Lily promised. "I guess old Travis just had some things he wanted to say and knew he might never again have such a grand opportunity." Somehow the thought made her sad.

Later, when they exited the sanctuary, Travis again met them, this time at the door. Lily extended her hand to him, and he grasped it. "It's been good to see you," she said. "Same here," he answered and laughed a nervous laugh. There was nothing more to say.

Lily went home that night and put on a pretty blue nightgown. She pulled back the covers and sat on the edge of the bed for a few moments while she connected herself to the oxygen under which she slept every night. She put on the cannula, attached tubing from the reservoir to the portable unit, and set the flow at 2 so that oxygen would be delivered only when she inhaled. Next she picked up from the nightstand the framed photograph of James. For a long time, she gazed at the photo, then pressed it briefly to her lips. "You were the right one for me," she whispered aloud. "I wish you were still here." The year of his illness and death had been the worst of her life.

She returned the photo to its usual place, then stretched out on the bed and tried to sleep but her mind kept flitting from one thing to another and one person to another—from James to Travis and back again. Silently she said her prayers. She prayed for her family and friends, especially for the well-being of her daughter and grandchildren, and she asked God's forgiveness for having lied that very night and for not being sorry she'd lied. Next she said the Lord's Prayer and the Twenty-Third Psalm. Afterwards, still restless, she repeated in her mind some poetry she'd memorized years ago. But too many memories were in the room; they were filling the room, all the crowded furniture of her life, so many people who had touched her life.

Finally she let her mind roam at will, let it carry her back in time to another house in another town and a bedroom where on spring nights with Travis beside her and the attic fan whirring and the big window open high, a sweet breeze would slip through the room and over their bodies like a friendly spirit.

Outside that big window, a gardenia bush bloomed each spring for a short while, its lush petals pure white and its leaves shiny as if they'd been dipped in oil. On warm spring nights, the fan pulled into the room the heavy scent of blossoms and dampness, and the scent merged with those of the room and the two people in it. And the shadows in the moonlight became a blur of two bodies, mouths and hands and arms and legs and youth and loving and, finally, miracle of miracles, a perfect child, their April.

Let it go, Lily told herself now. *Sleep. I need to sleep. There's still tomorrow, after all...something to do, someplace to go.* Then the night sounds slipped around her. And she closed her eyes in darkness. And a shawl of silence wrapped around her and soothed her with softness. And just beyond that cotton-wool world, that twilight place—the pulse of the oxygen, the throb of life, lulled and comforted at each inhalation.

Betty Davis   *Houston*

THE LAKE

The lake seeped into my soul,
like a live Renoir, flaunting
soft colors on a summer day.

Bright berries and wild roses
grew like a fringed border
where water stroked the earth.
Showy against the sky-blue surface,
dark, green branches swayed in air
filled with the sweetness of cedar.

This lake was born of love.
Granny's legacy used to fashion
the dam father dreamed and built.

My roots are there, will always
be attached to the vine I am
rambling round the world
where my mind takes me, places
that pique my interest, but
can never have my heart.

Betty Davis   *Houston*

OLD—WHATEVER THAT IS

In a honky-tonk on Route 66, 1941,
dark corners filled with excitement,
dim lights, dancing to Harry James songs
that smiled into unfilled hearts
ready to swing, ready to sing.
There was an air of the future
a place where dreams
would write new songs, new dances,
but for now, let the jitterbug reign.
We had no need for tomorrow
waiting out there like our parents
waited our maturity, inevitable
irrepressible, a constant yeast.
Everything wonderful and terrible
happened in those unfolding years
until now, that finds the dancers
still with unfilled hearts waiting,
ready to dance, ready to sing
to a world that calls them old,
whatever that is. They have felt
all the changes ring in their bones
and rock in their minds until 1998
when a sweet jazz is the only thing
that can make them smile. The air
of this future, here and now, excites,
nurtures love of the spiritual
and frees the old to be young still,
to write new songs, dance new dances.

Juanita Gibson

TOMORROW'S GONNA BE A WONDERFUL DAY

Tiny shafts of sunbeams found their way through thick foliage, past briars and yaupon to ground covered with rotting leaves and pine needles. Rabbit trails zigzagged into thick briars and deer paths wound through yaupon thickets. Feral hogs frequented the area, leaving behind torn up ground and wallowing bogs. Tender May Apple plants pushed through the natural mulch of the forest floor in search of life-giving sunlight. Thick green moss and mushrooms grew in the deep shade.

A narrow road wound its way through these dense woods, its once smooth black-top surface now pock marked with ragged holes. Large areas of paving material had long since worn away, leaving a road bed of deep sand. Limbs from large oaks and tall pines extended overhead, creating a leafy tunnel through the East Texas woods.

A pick-up truck, its bed enclosed with ply-wood side-boards, bounced and rattled over the rough surfaced road. Rick had spent his life here and knew every crook and turn of the road. He was an expert at evading the pot holes and staying in the deep sandy ruts of the un-paved areas. He enjoyed the challenge and drove with wild abandon. A rabbit darted across the road in front of the truck. Rick laughed raucously, "Missed him," He shouted.

Tonya tried to keep her mind distracted as the old truck careened through the forest. "There's my tree, " she said to herself as they passed a pine tree with a large thick clump of needles on a lower limb. There were several trees along the road that she liked but the pine was her favorite, standing so tall and proud. For some reason it gave her comfort to see the tree, silently reaching out its limbs to her.

She smiled to herself, then glanced at Rick to see if he had noticed her smile.

"What're you looking at?" he growled.

"Nothin'," she mumbled, "I ain't lookin at nothin'."

"Don't get smart with me, woman," his hand was quick and Tonya felt the blood as it trickled from her nose. His hands were huge and strong and she knew better than say anything more. To fight back was unthinkable and would bring grim consequences.

She sat in silence as a lone tear rolled down her cheek. She must be careful, he hated her crying. Tears only brought more blows, inflicted to "stop her crying." She quietly sniffed and kept her eyes straight ahead. It really didn't matter what she did. She could never please him. She was "dammed if she did and dammed if she didn't."

"Now, you better straighten up, we're almost to Jim and Claire's. Wipe that hurt look off your face. You ain't hurt none. I mean it now, woman, straighten up."

Tonya wiped the blood from her nose. She pulled down the sun visor and looked into the small mirror. She smoothed her tousled dark hair and touched her injured nose.

Rick turned the pickup into a narrow drive and stopped by a white picket fence. A man dressed in blue overalls stood by the yard gate.

His voice was gruff as he yelled toward the house, "Claire, get out here. They're here." He smiled at his guests, "Ya'll get out and come on in. Shore is gonna be a good night fer fishing. The almanac even says so. Yeah, we'll have a fine ole' time."

Claire hurried across the yard. She was an older version of Tonya with the same shining dark hair and sky blue eyes. She wore cut-off jeans, a plaid shirt and was bare footed.

She nodded to Rick and turned to her sister."Hi, Little Baby Sister. Come on, let's go in the house and get us a nice cold glass of lemonade."

The two men headed for the beer cooler in the barn. Claire and Tonya went into the house. Claire served the lemonade then tenderly touched her sister's face.

"Oh, Tonny, what's that SOB done to you this time? Just look at you."

"I'm OK, Claire, I'll be all right. But I've been thinking about what we talked about.. Do you really think it'll work?"

"Child, we have to be real careful but everything's gonna be fine. Don't worry, it's all taken care of. We just have to be cool and keep our heads."

Supper was waiting when the men came into the house, fried chicken, mashed potatoes, fresh green beans, biscuits, cream gravy and tall glasses of iced tea. A freshly baked cake waited on the sideboard, a cake with 'special' chocolate icing.

"Ummmmm, I'm hongry as a bear," said Jim. "Here, Rick, pull up a chair and sit yerself down. We ain't got much but try to make out yer supper."

The two men sat at the table and hungrily devoured the food as fast as the women could refill the bowls. The sisters waited on the table, refilled the biscuit platter and poured more gravy. Claire served large slices of the chocolate cake.

When supper was over, Rick and Jim loaded their fishing gear into Jim's truck, placing it in the back with the wooden skiff and oars. They were off to the lake for their weekly fishing trip.

The sisters sat on the front porch and watched the truck disappear down the drive.

After awhile Tonya sighed. "This is nice…so peaceful. Look, there's a lightening bug, there in the edge of the woods. Remember when we used to catch'em and put 'em in fruit jars?"

Claire nodded. "Yeah, we had fun when we were little."

They watched the last rays of sunlight fade and stars appear one by one in the darkening sky. They heard whip-poor-wills calling in the deep woods, and saw the moon rise through the trees and begin its nightly journey across the starlit sky. A lone mockingbird sang its plaintive song from the top of the pear tree in the yard.

At last, Claire rose from her chair, "Come on, Little Sister, it's close to ten o'clock. Let's go in and watch the news."

The newscaster announced the lead story, "The bodies of two local men were recovered from the lake tonight. Names have not been released pending notification of next of kin."

Claire smiled and hugged Tonya . "Come on, hon, let's turn in. It's getting late and we need our beauty sleep. After all, tomorrow's gonna be a wonderful day."

Guida Jackson   *The Woodlands*

GOATHEAD

Floyd was grubbing weeds near the northern boundary of his quarter-section when a cloud of dust from the road stopped and hovered over the house. Probably that damn sprinkler salesman. The numbskull was stubborn as bindweed. Floyd had spent the better part of the daylight hours one afternoon explaining how he prided himself on being a dryland farmer, one of the few holdouts in Donley County.

Dryland farming was an art, he tried to get through to that spikey-haired dimwit, a technique handed from father to son as long as people had been cultivating this arid sandy soil that was perfect for storing capillary water. The trick, he instructed as the salesman's eyes glazed over, is to plow deep after a rain, break up the soil as fine as possible to increase its capacity to hold moisture, and then compact the top to make a dust mulch that prevents water from escaping. Conservation at its finest, he'd said, maybe boasting a little, but the salesman only launched off into something about easy payment plans. Young fool probably took one look at the one-bedroom house with its rotting porch and figured he couldn't afford sprinklers.

He was right, of course. And no amount of promises of bounteous crops would entice Floyd to step off into a gulch he couldn't see the bottom of.

The bell rang up at the house: Hazel's signal to come home. Floyd frowned at the half-finished furrow, then started for his pickup. Must be something important. Hazel would never call him in to talk to a maggoty salesman. He tossed the hoe into the pickup bed, got into the old crate, cranked her up and rumbled back to the house.

Before he got there, he recognized Cal Whatley's new Ex-Cab Silverado parked in the yard. "What now?" he muttered, slowing to a creep. Whatley's section abutted on the north, and seemed like every time Floyd turned around, his neighbor was over with a new complaint.

With great reluctance he got out and went inside, where Hazel was nervously trying to entertain this yahoo with the fresh store-bought haircut. Whatley rose from the sofa, his full height and girth—and Aqua-Velva—filling the room.

"Morning, Floyd," he said, extending a white-nailed paw.

Floyd took his time removing his dusty hat, slapping it across his leg a couple of times, then wiping his palm down his side before shaking. Man ought to be ashamed of himself having soft white hands that never did a lick of work.

"What brings you this time, Cal?"

Hazel seemed to jump at his tone; maybe he sounded a bit too combative. She gripped her reddened knuckles in front of her in desperate entreaty. "Why don't you all sit down. Can I fix you some ice tea?"

Cal's eyes didn't leave Floyd's face. "None for me, thanks. I just got up from the breakfast table."

It was all Floyd could do to keep from snorting out loud. If he'd had a watch he'd have made a great show of checking the time. Floyd had already put in a half-day's work while this pissant was parked on the can reading the paper.

Both men remained standing as Whatley said, "I stopped by to see what you plan to do about the goatheads. Every time there's a south wind, they blow over, take root and about choke out my Milo."

"Maybe if your rows wasn't so wet, the goatheads wouldn't take such good ahold." Floyd plopped into his rocker and felt Hazel's glare, so he added, "Matter of fact, I was out there just now, hoeing them out, back along your fenceline."

The big man remained standing, legs planted apart, hardly a wrinkle in the Haband slacks above the polished boots. What kind of farmer wears Haband pants, Floyd thought. Hazel retreated to the kitchen door where she lurked, ready to be summoned at any moment to provide sustenance.

"Chopping's not getting the job done, Floyd. You might ought to consider a weed eradicator."

Floyd propped one foot on the other knee and counted to ten—well, four, at least. "What you trying to do? Wipe out what little chance I got to make a dab of profit on my cotton?"

Whatley shrugged and smiled behind bland eyes. "You got to spend a little to make anything. You know that."

Floyd didn't intend to be lectured in his own home. "Is that all you come about?"

"No, I guess not." Whatley perched on the end of the sofa closest to Floyd, his long legs extending so far, their knees almost touched. "We been having this same conversation for several years now and nothing's come of it. So I've decided to offer to buy you out."

Hazel gasped and took a tentative step into the front room. Floyd shot her a frown, and she retreated. But there was a glint of hope in her eyes.

Whatley pulled a check from his shirt pocket and handed it over. "I even brought earnest money, as show of good faith."

As Floyd took the check, all he could see was the dirt under his own finger-nails. He fished his glasses from a pile of bills on the side table so he could read the numbers. Five thousand dollars. He reckoned it was good. He studied the check for a long time, thinking about their future, his and Hazel's. He was sixty-eight. What would they do when he couldn't work anymore?

As if reading his mind, Cal said, "You and Hazel could stay on in this house so long as you live. Hazel could keep her chickens, and you could plant that garden patch out back. I'd even deed it to you for life."

He knew what Hazel was thinking. Selling would solve all their worries. No more watching the sky for dust clouds or hail storms or late spring northers, no fretting about goatheads or bindweed or boll weevils. No repairing fences with arthritic fingers. No plowing, no harrowing, no harvesting. No jerry-rigged repairs on the old tractor, that he sometimes got so mad at, he whacked it with his pliers and cursed the name of Allis-Chalmers to high heaven. They would be free to do as they pleased, maybe visit their daughter in California. He'd always wanted to see California before he died.

He dragged his gaze up to meet Hazel's pleading one, sweeping past the photo of his father on the wall near the kitchen door, imagining his dad saying, Go on, be the grasshopper on Cal's mud-flap. Lordy, women made things so godawful hard.

At length he rose, shaking his head. He wouldn't feel right turning over this land to somebody with hands like a ticket-taker at the Tilta-Whirl.

He didn't look at Hazel again. It was painful to watch a woman cry. Finally, he pocketed the check, sighing.

"Tell you what. If you call the FSA and find out the fair market value, you can have it for that."

Whatley beamed in astonishment. "Sure thing."

Floyd headed for the door before he had to shake hands again. "Now I got to get back to my goatheads." Then he turned to add, "Ever notice how much a goathead looks like the head of a horny toad? Horny toads are just about extinct, I heard. Starved out by crop dusters. But we got plenty around here."

He left the house grinning. Soon as the deal was signed and they had their money, he knew exactly what he'd plant in his garden: Row upon row of nothing but goatheads.

Leona Welch   *Denison*

DEATH IDENTIFIED

Lost in shadows of a drugged
dream world
she does not remember her name–

Those who recognize her stumbling stagger
laughing when she does
have nicknamed her Dizzy

There are some who take advantage
of her vacant state of mind–
without permission, they
pillage her body and pilfer her cart
leaving little to trade and barter

so she makes the dizzy rounds again
digging out recyclables
begging nickels at the traffic light
because her 'work for food' sign was stolen . . .

Death comes in small measured doses–
with trembling fingers
she plunges the discarded needle into
broken bruised veins

and waits

for the promised high
which whirls her beyond the horror
she knows as home
where names have no meaning–

Patricia Pecorello Hilborn   *Haslet*

STRANGERS ON A PLANE

The night we met, she was coffee bar hopping with friends, playing bored princess with everyone who spoke to her. That included me, a short guy who liked a short leash, but at the time I couldn't see past the curve of hips beneath her clingy red skirt. I swam in her deep brown eyes, my boxer shorts bunched, but she never looked at me clutching my oversized mug, hiding in my day-dream, letting the coffee's steam cloud my eyes. After buying a cappuccino from the tattooed teen ogling her behind the counter, she walked my way, balancing her mug with one hand, dropping a handful of change into her purse with the other. She bumped into my table and slung coffee drops off her wrist in my direction. I caught the drops in midair, to the roar of an imaginary but appreciative crowd. The coffee sizzled on my fingers. A few landed on my scone. After frowning at my choice of dessert, she accepted my hand-signaled invitation to stay. I accepted half of her biscotti, a crunchy slice of her heart.

Her eyes danced as she recited her story, dangling something, maybe inter-est, at me. When I leaned in for a closer look, she blinked the clues away. Her family raised cotton in Central Texas and she spent most of her youth working the fields alongside migrants. She never finished high school, but was chosen at twenty-five to attend an MFA program in Vermont and became an award-winning journalist.

She'd made it up, of course. But watching her mouth curl at the edges, I wanted to believe. With a sweep of her fingers, she'd flip her brown hair over her shoulder and I wanted to touch her exposed earlobes. She'd pick a crumb off her blouse and I wanted to eat it.

When we'd finished the biscotti, she shrugged me off and left with her girls. As the door closed behind them, I overheard someone call her Marianne.

For weeks, I haunted the coffee house. After all, the place was mine before it was ours. I took up smoking again. I deserted my chess club. Alone at my table, sipping latte, a halved biscotti waiting for her, I'd hum a song from the sixties, one of my old man's favorites, changing the name in my head. *Hey, Marianne . . .*

The Friday night she breezed through the door, I understood why her clothes clung to her so. They wanted to. Her black T-shirt stopped short of her wide leather belt, exposing a sliver of waistline as she reached for the mug. She neared my table, her glance sweeping past my face, down my arm. I pushed the biscotti toward her.

She stopped. "Sharing that with someone?"

Another man might look back at that starter's-signal moment and wonder why she took the chair I offered. Another man might regret making the offer. But I had to know if I could play her game. She took the biscotti.

Week one. She lied about changing her phone number. Week two. She denied mailing unsigned cards, postage due, to my home. Week three. The manager at Trader's Book Mart told me to stop following Marianne down the aisles, which I was, because she'd complained we'd never been formally introduced, which we hadn't. I tipped him five to do so.

Our first real dinner date, she showed up late and tried to pass off an elderly Italian woman as her mother. Lots of Italians immigrated to Texas in the 1930s, she told me. Signora Marasco giggled behind her black shawl while I blubbered hello. Disintegrating into laughter, Marianne doubled over, losing her nose ring under the table. A ten-minute search on our knees turned up nothing. Not even her real mother.

When she moved into my place, I prayed I wouldn't lose myself.

While I cooked, she'd hover over the sauce pan, dipping in the last of my bread crust, tasting me in my mother's recipe.

"I'll let you know when it's done," I'd tell her. "Set the table."

One place setting would appear, the fork rolled inside a paper towel. She'd pull her chair alongside mine, waiting, a smolder in her eyes. I'd toss some meatballs and a large scoop of rigatoni on the plate, and hand over my fork. Marianne wasn't stingy. She never ate the last meatball. Afterward, she quenched my appetite by sharing a close-quartered shower. Twenty minutes of soulful cuddling completed the drill.

I let her cheat at Parcheesi and drank her warmed-over coffee laced with red wine. The vinegary sting brought tears to my eyes. I wondered what was behind hers. Always, she had a new story. The time she worked for the CIA. The Pulitzer prize- winning author who'd stolen her idea. The religious sect that wanted to find her. The fog would lift for a moment when she'd talk about bread, food of the soul she called it. I started bringing home extra loaves — Italian, sourdough, marbled rye.

In July I had to leave her. Four times a year, the home office ordered me to Seattle for a weekend of drinks and reprimands. I broke the news with a fresh baguette. Marianne said she'd have to go to the coffee house alone. Maybe she'd throw out the Parcheesi board. She needed to find a new bakery.

I surprised her with a plane ticket.

Before I could tell her the plan, she grabbed the computerized slip and compared it to my own Seattle itinerary, nodding with each concurrence.

"I'll have to drink with your boss?"

"You can visit the coffee shops instead."

"You'll be reprimanded?"

"We'll be strangers on a plane."

That odd quizzical look, the one I'd seen in May, replaced her skeptical frown. She tilted her head.

"Our seats are together, see?" Pointing at the tickets, I stumbled through the details. "But we'll arrive at the airport in separate cabs, check in at different times and pretend we don't know each other."

"We'll meet again," she said, her eyes gone vacant. I'd seen her this way before, moving about the coffee house, careless with her steaming mug, observing desperate men, being observed by them. Without consenting, she pulled her ratty beige Samsonite carry-on from the hall closet, and started packing.

The rest of the week, she ate on her own plate. She didn't share the shower. When she abstained from bread on Sunday, I worried. But that night, well, she made it up to me.

"So we can remember how it used to be. Before we start over," she whispered, her breath hot on my neck.

I remembered to breathe.

The next morning I took a cab to DFW International, alone. Marianne joined the check-in line as I stepped through the doors to the boarding ramp. Her sunglasses balanced on the end of her nose, she peered at the departure signs, ignoring my wink. The side of her mouth didn't even twitch.

A stewardess showed my stranger to our row in first class. During takeoff, Marianne flipped through the in-flight magazine, her midriff peeking beneath a T-shirt. Remembering the night before, I tried a smile in her direction. Her eyes threw back darts the way they did when I took too long at Parcheesi. As the ground shrank beneath us, the stewardess stopped at Marianne's elbow.

"Vodka and tonic." She exhaled her order like smoke from an expensive cigar, her lips curving around the words. I just managed to keep from laughing. Maybe I was jealous. She'd never breathed my name like that.

The stewardess nodded, a whiff of indulgence on her face, and took my request for coffee, black. Marianne watched our brief exchange, her eyes narrowing. As the slim figure walked toward the galley, I turned to my travel companion to introduce myself. Marianne's glance, full of moth-balled indifference, cut me short.

When the drinks arrived, Marianne knocked back a good swallow and set the glass on the edge of her tray, tipping some of the clear liquid onto my left wrist. She brushed the droplets off her knee, her cold gaze meeting my friendly-guy smile.

"Can I buy you a new drink?" I asked, wishing for a chocolate-dipped biscotti to edge her way.

Marianne studied me for a moment, regrouping, changing her mind on the fly. "You know, I shouldn't be drinking this early anyway. My doctor told me to lay off, under the circumstances."

She described her mild heart condition, about flying home to Seattle to say goodbye to her father, a recent movie deal on her third novel. Like a slice of day-old bread, I soaked up every lie, not wanting to hurry her, mesmerized. She paused to take a breath and raised an eyebrow.

"You don't believe me."

"Yes. Yes I do." I leaned toward her, touching her hand. Her skin felt cool, thin. I had imagined the heat. "Marianne, I believe every word you're saying."

Jerking away, she rubbed my touch off her fingers with a cocktail napkin, buffing red circles on her skin. I realized we hadn't been introduced. How could I have slipped so soon?

After two unsteady tries, Marianne stood, knocking the vodka onto the cabin floor. She reached for her handbag, stepped away from our row and away from my outstretched hand.

My smile froze as she launched into an uneven recap of her life with the guy sitting behind me. He ate up the Seattle story, letting her talk, probably nodding when she paused for emphasis, like I should have.

I stirred my lukewarm coffee, reviewing my flawed attempts at finding a woman who did not want to be found, who traded bread crumbs for sustenance. Staring out the window at the clouds crowding the sky, I wondered if the Seattle airport had a bakery. When the plane touched down, Marianne made her way to the front, leaning on the arm of our fellow passenger, his conservative tie loosened. I kept my smile intact, rehearsing a lie of my own. But her eyes never met mine.

D. Phelps   *Bulverde*

HATCHING

Having broken through the
cold, white shell of winter, my
soul stretches its sparrow neck,
demands a feeding, still wet and
open throated

HOLLOWING BACK

Made heavy with moisture of
memory, I lay me down like fallen
oak on forest floor; wait for earth to
hollow me back to the black of my
beginning, root and grow me over with
covering vines

Christopher Woods   *Houston*

GOODBYE AT THE RIVERSIDE

Launching your bier
In the muddy water,
We begin singing,
Our voices strident
As gulls
Round a shrimper
Bound for evening port.

We sing for you,
For a lost part of ourselves
Gone drifting.

You will ride this stream
To the sea
And beyond
If our faith is strong.
Water, now muddy,
Will become blue,
Wider than the eye.

Soon, you will know
The magic of passage.
How all whitecaps
Become clouds
That measure your progress
Across the sky.

Wesley Riddle *Belton*

SPANISH MOSS

Spanish moss seemed to cover my Southern sweet and old hometown,
which I loved long and grew up in, then grew out of with dumb luck.

That stuff stuck to green and deadwood and hung like cotton flocked
onto tree branches, its shadow cast on old eyelids and younger hands.

Black moss we called it, clinging to every place like a thick phlegm,
sticking to hidden parts, outside in dark woods and inside our hearts.

We looked askance there at a black man, in suit or rags: paid no mind,
whether he were on a bus or in a want ad, or drawn on wanted posters;

simply he were black. No equal expectation allowed, and none tried;
no expectation at all really, just a prickly kind of fear and great desire

to enlarge the distance or to lay steel tracks between us, to erect walls.
Funny, I don't even recall ever planting or cultivating that damn moss.

It just sort of grew without normal roots, more akin to webs attached
at corners in lofts and attics, where all black spiders have already died.

Akin as well to polyps breathed in that start to consume a healthy lung.
Spanish moss hung alright, draped like a lynching, narrowing open sky.

And if I've managed any perspective from age and experience, those
cruel teachers have tempered soul and tossed self-righteousness aside

hopefully anyway: seen in the camera of my mind the great enormity,
oddly juxtaposed to some still beautiful things, wondering how it came

to pass and stayed with us so long, like a bout with feverish sickness,
like moss choking my magnolias, smothering out the fragrant blossoms.

Strange symbiosis twixt striped aching backs and pineapples silver gilt:
violence and hospitality, dainty milk white shoulders and black belt soil,

and soiled black men. Things surreally attractive in the dim red shades
of late twilight, reckoning what the moss mostly did-obscured a vision:

hid blue loss of true redemption, the carried cross, what might have been,
but kept hid too our view of the Promised Land, from off this mountain top.

Naomi Stroud Simmons   *Fort Worth*

THE SERMON

Betty and I were buying popcorn
at the *Tom Mix Saturday Matinee*
when Kaye showed us the box

of kittens behind the counter.
Her mom told her to get rid of them.
   Honor thy Father and thy Mother

After the movie, when Betty's dad
picked us up, we were ten-year-old happy
with our squirming tabby, took it to Betty's house,

dressed it in doll clothes, then
knew her mother would not be able
to resist it; the other cats would

help take care of it.
In the kitchen with steam
from dinner shining her face

she took one glance:
     Go drown that damn cat in the pond!
   Honor thy Father and thy Mother

As the soft fur floated and all
was still, we made plans for a funeral.
Since I killed the cat, Betty held the service.

Her mother preached the sermon.

Janice Rose

MISS ANNIE'S GIFT

Miss Polly was six-years-old when President Abraham Lincoln was assassinated. Her father was an AWOL-prisoner in the Civil War on Bald Head Island, N.C. where he died. Later, Miss Polly's common-law husband was a relative of General Robert E. Lee.

I stood in her doorway when I was six watching you feed Miss Polly, your mother, then ninety. She sat upright in her featherbed and spat saliva full of stringbeans into your face and eyeglasses. You laid the spoon down on her plate and sat them on the floor slowly lifting the lap of your apron to wipe, to cleanse it all off. You said nothing. But kept on filling the spoon to feed her mashed potatoes and overcooked shreds of chicken. Miss Polly, my great-grandmother, was toothless then except for one long gold-capped tooth gleaming when she opened her mouth. I remember the way her mouth and tongue circled food around that nugget-tooth like some huge granary wheel confined in a corn mill. She rarely spoke to me, but once broke off a sweet gum twig for me to chew on—the pioneer's toothbrush. Even when she cursed you and called you vile names...names that titilated my young ears, you never spoke back in anger or calculated vengeance. You kept on getting her dressed in one of her ankle-length, long-sleeved, calico dresses; pulled up those thick cotton-flesh stockings which you gartered around her knees, or sometimes rolled down around her ankles. You gently guided her feet into black oxford heels that you laced and tied with wide arc bows. Slowly brushing her gray hair still lined with strawberry streaks, you pulled and hairpinned it into a knotted bun on her nape. Miss Polly felt undressed without her starched white cotton apron that you sashed around her thickened waist. In earlier years when she left the house, before taking to her bed in deafness and lost sight, she wore a broad-brimmed bonnet for protection from the sun and prying eyes. She'd walk with her cane in one hand and you on the other arm. Miss Polly never learned to read or write and when the Philco was on, she *watched* the radio. She insisted that you keep a broom under the front porch steps to keep witches away. And since she rarely wore pierced earrings, she pushed a broomstraw in each ear lobe to keep the Devil from coming through. Miss Polly died in the summer of 1951. Not long after, my uncle opened her weathered-pine travel trunk that smelled of dried mint, mothballs, snuff and Tums, picked up her gleaming gold tooth and dropped it in his pocket.

Joe M. O'Connell *Austin*

A LITTLE TONGUE

I've seen things. Damn right. Try living out here and not seeing. Got to keep your eyes open and moving. Take Dumpsters. I find all kinds of arty-facts in Dumpsters. Of course, you got your garden variety trash—newspapers, plastic, old Jell-O. Screw that. You want something with value, something you can sell if you can't eat it. I found a tongue once. It was small and squishy. Maybe a baby's tongue. No I did not eat it, if that's what you're thinking, you sick puppy. I bet a cat did though; they'll eat just about anything.

See things? I see it all. Easy when you're invisible. They walk past me like I'm a dog or a burning cigarette butt somebody forgot to step on. She walked past me every day. I didn't know her name, but I called her Melissa because I'd always thought that was pretty. The thing about
Melissa is she was lonely. You could tell. She'd walk with her head low, arms swinging at her sides. Like she was somebody in a hurry, but I knew she just didn't want to talk. Self-imposed loneliness.

I figure Melissa worked in a bank. Wore those dark suits the bankers like, only they looked good on Melissa. Had style. She drank cappuccino and ate exotic foods like squid.

Click click click, her shoes went on the sidewalk. I was squatting by the newspaper rack collecting my thoughts. Damned if she didn't slip her quarters in right next to me. Getting a Wall Street Journal, all businesslike. She smiled at me and I noticed her name tag said Stephanie.
You could tell Stephanie had style by the way she slid that newspaper under her arm. Heavenly.

I imagined a whole life for Stephanie. She went out with this guy, Gary. He was some kind of salesman, cars or insurance. Something where he made the big bucks, but you could tell he wasn't really in Stephanie's league. Yeah, one day she'd wise up and dump him.
Stephanie grew up doing what everybody expected. Everything. Her whole life. In high school she was in the debate club, head cheerleader, a state silver medallist in the high hurdles, senior class treasurer, and she volunteered after school twice a week at the veterans' hospital. Emptying bedpans. It makes me shudder to think about it. Her parents were proud as could be.

She was a good girl, Stephanie was. Didn't lose her virginity till she was nineteen and a sophomore at state college. She had a scholarship from the Knights of Columbus. Yeah, nice Catholic girl. She gave her cherry to a senior named Steve Wolchoski, a smooth operator she used to tutor in basic math. Wolchoski played the guitar and read her some poetry that he said he wrote just for her. He copied it out of a library book. Robert Frost, Emily Dickinson, some big name's lesser works. Nobody's the wiser and it's reusable. "I feel like

I can tell you my true feelings, Stephanie. I feel so vulnerable with you. Hold me." What a loser. He died in a car wreck three years later. Or was it AIDS? No one's sure.

Anyway, Stephanie got over it and found herself a genuine nice guy. Robert Smith, a bland white bread boring slab of a kid. Chemistry major with plans for medical school. It lasted two sleepy years. Stephanie was sweetheart of his fraternity—no big feat with the dogs those stiffs dated.

She broke it off without hurting his feelings too badly. "We've grown apart, Robby." He hardly saw her anyway. She worked three days a week at the homeless shelter, was president of the accounting club, recording secretary of the Young Republicans and baked cookies for the Cub Scouts. She made one 'B' in four years. Nearly killed her that 'B' did. In economics. The professor was a Yugoslavian who counseled Middle Eastern countries on world finance issues. Stephanie couldn't hardly understand a word the foreign big shot said. Too polite to mention it, bless her heart.

The summer after graduation she interned at the United Nations. New-By-Gawd-York City. It blew her mind. Her mother tried to talk her out of it. Stephanie grew up in a small town. Population—2,563. Major industry—farming and the sixth largest aglet factory in the world. Climate—moderate, with occasional flurries. She was not prepared in the least for the Big Apple, Mommy said, tying those apron strings around her little girl's neck. Figuratively, I mean. Daddy was the one who turned the tide. He was a honcho at the aglet factory. Head of the athletics division. Once went to a convention in Dallas and found it only mildly shocking. New experiences would broaden the baby girl's horizons. You only live once. Ha cha cha while the ha cha chaing is good.

She shared an efficiency apartment with a friend of her cousin. The girl's name was Desiree and she was studying acting at some private workshop, the method bunk where you pretend you're a potato for three hours a day.

By daylight, Stephanie was translating press releases (she was fluent in Spanish and Farsi) and keeping the coffee cups filled. At night, Desiree introduced her to The Scene. The nightclubs, leather, punks with attitudes, artists, pseudo-artists, gays, Jews, closet stockbrokers, Armenian food. She ate it all up. When you're that age, who needs sleep? She burned the candle at both ends and it was a Roman candle.

It was out partying at some basement glitter bar that she met Forentzo, a performance artist with a loft in Soho. His parents were dirt poor but both sets of grandparents were rolling in the dough and kept F. comfortable. He never told Stephanie his last name, but she would have recognized it if he did. Filthy, he was. I mean he was comfortable, but he wasn't much of a bather either, so you could go by that definition too.

Stephanie was finishing up her internship when she ran into the tattered Forentzo. Desiree (that week she was an asparagus) dragged her to this art opening at Counterfeit Prom and there he was. In a cage above their heads wearing nothing but banana skins and clipping his toenails with his teeth. When he saw Stephanie, he howled at the moon for fifteen minutes straight.

Stephanie could respect a man committed to his art. He slipped her a banana skin with his address on it and "8 p.m. tomorrow, my hut?"

Their date consisted of roaming the streets giving out chewing gum to street persons. But F. really won Stephanie's heart when he pulled a can of spray paint out of his trench coat and wrote: "Stephanie Is My Everlovin' Sex Goddess and I Love Her So Much It Hurts" on the sides of a taxi cab while the driver dozed inside. Later that night they broke into Counterfeit Prom and made like love chimps in F.'s little cage. At six in the morning, Stephanie crawled out with the spray paint and wrote "Forentzo's Underarms Have Cotton Candy Hair" above the bar. The manager knew art when he saw it and framed it later that night. The critic from the Times called it "New Industrial Kitsch with an edge."

Desiree was leaving on a six-month tour of the Midwest with "Stoned Again," a musical revival of early Rolling Stones-pre-Jerry Hall. Desiree spent the first act wearing a giant thumb costume. The pay was good.

Stephanie decided to move in with F., whom she found out let anybody he met, including the gum-chewing street people, sleep in his living room for months at a time. But, hey, Stephanie was loosening up. She discovered cocaine and its good buddy crank and dropped a few pounds, even though she was already a svelte sweet thing, if you ask me.

One night, F. talked her into shaving all the hair off her body.

"Let's go back into the womb," he said. Easy for him, he had a walk-up.

Stephanie woke up at noon with her heart running in full throttle in the turn stretch with Al Unser Jr. riding up on her rear. When she calmed down, she discovered it was really a wino fondling her posterior section.

The fellow traveler smiled a toothless grin and started whistling "Dixie." Stephanie didn't know what to think; she'd always heard Southerners were gentlemen.

F. was nowhere to be found. Two weeks later Stephanie had helped most of the homeless squatters find alternative shelter (with an ample supply of Juicy Fruit) and found herself alone with prickly heat and a bloody nose in an apartment that smelled of dirty socks. She broke down and cried. Then she poured black paint onto F.'s art-deco furniture and used her fingers to write obscene love letters to the missing monkey boy. She sold the inscribed furniture to some friends who ran a trendy gallery.

It occasionally pops up in revivals of Post-Druid Breakfast Nook art. Stephanie spent the cash for an Eva Gabor wig, five business suits and a plane ticket to here. She knocked unannounced on the door of her college roommate, Debbie Venture, a cute little redhead who majored in sports medicine but now was a salesperson for an inflatable furniture company.

Debbie's new husband answered the door and grinned for ear to ear. It took Stephanie a minute to realize this was her old buddy Wolchoski, who had grown a few extra chins and a sizable beer gut since last she'd spit in his direction. Did I say he was dead before? No, that was somebody else. He and Debbie had met up on the road when she tried to push an inflatable footstool his way and he tried to interest her in junk bonds. The marriage was bound to succeed, if only for the tax shelters involved.

Stephanie spent about three weeks sleeping on the Wolchoski's couch. One night she awoke to Steve-o towering over her like an animated Bob's Big Boy. She calmly removed the scarf from her nubby skull, grabbed the W.'s wedding picture and broke it across Steve's face, doing her best Sinead O'Connor: "Fight the real enemy."

Fortunately, the bank job came through. By the time Stephanie's hair had grown in she was halfway up the corporate ladder and climbing. F. sent her a letter once, addressed to general mail and postmarked from Nashville. It was a series of strips of paper ripped from fast food napkins and mixed at random. Every time Stephanie read them the message was different. Once it was, "Dogs are fine parboiled but don't forget the Alamo loves you like a brother." Another time it was, "Baby, I'm a gonna hiss like it's yesterday's show beats rubbing yak parts down Highway 57 Revisited."

I think she's gotten over him. Last week she gave me a dollar and smiled at me. Yes sir, that's one executive you won't find out back Dumpster diving, fighting for the wilted lettuce. I think she's bound for the top once she dumps that latest sleazy boyfriend, Gary. Ask his parents. He's been nothing but trouble from the start. It all began in kindergarten when he dropped a tack in the teacher's chair without her noticing. Oh, I could tell you stories about Gary. By the way, man, you got a dollar?

Neal Ostman   *Colleyville*

Rue Saint Hillarie

Dishes clatter, flatware rings,
punctuating a low level hubbub
of murmurs and laughter.
     Dark-eyed busboys snatch away
     with raptor-like moves,
     sauce-soaked and gristle remains.

Lithe virginal bloused waitresses,
narrow butt waiters
gather at their stations, then
pad among the patrons,
solicit, convey and befriend.

Foods move allegro,
conducted in swift gestures
darting looks
and head nods from
the blue-suited man;
managing—to stuff
the bankers.

Janet McCann   *Bryan/College Station*

JUNIOR YEAR ABROAD
(For Sondra)

You sent me black French underwear,
sleek wisps, a filmy slip, bikini briefs
and a lush lace bra. How much unlike my
holey fruit-of-the-looms. I put them on,
ran my hands over them and dreamed,
Jean-Claude, Louis, Jacques, René, François
drifted into our dorm room like blue smoke.

But they didn't take, they itched, tight second skin
I peeled away; I folded them tenderly
and put them in the drawer, behind my scented
Chinese scarves. I think I have them still.

Weeks from dying, you called me lucky,
one man, one home. I said that you would not
have liked my life, not really, and you laughed,
your old smile come back, your whole face
once more alight. *No, I had many men, and I
was very glad to have them, still more glad
to see them go*, you said.

William Virgil Davis   *Waco*

A NIGHT AGO

for Jim

There we were, at home together, the first time
in memory. It was winter and cold. New snow
had fallen past the windows during dinner
and we sat in silence, each deep in his own depths.
Then the long dark of the dark began in such
an unobtrusive way I only notice it now — how
many years later? Someone must have said
something to Jim, and, as was his way, he simply
stood, stilled for a moment, and then turned,
and the next thing any of us knew he was gone,
out into the night, somewhere no one would
ever know. I've often wondered where he went.

Then, halfway to morning, everyone long
in bed, I heard him come in and make his way
through the dark rooms we both knew by memory,
rooms I remember, as I imagine them again,
as accurately as anything I've ever known. He
came slowly up the stairs and entered the room
where I lay awake, listening and waiting, hoping
he would whisper something to me, so that I
could answer him out of the dark — even now,
after all of these years.

Alan Berecka   *Sinton*

CHILD REARING

"Just wait until your Father
gets home." An unwelcomed
mantra the boy's mother sung
often after his boyhood
transgressions were judged
too great for the metal end
of the fly swatter that hung
next to the bathroom door.

Banished to his bed,
the boy just waited
for the Father's return
and aged long years
each hour, as he waited
to hear crushed gravel groan
under the weight of braking tires,
waited for a rusted car door
to fall shut, waited for a garage
door to rumble open, waited
for the report of a the Father's tin
lunch pail against a kitchen screen
door , waited for the first heavy footfall
on the cold linoleum, waited
for the shrill question muted
by a houseful of walls, " Do you
know what your son did today?"

"Jeezus Key-riste, Woman,
don't start with me now,"
The Father's often ignored reply
went unnoticed as she repeated
the boy's trespasses with the zeal
of an Old Testament prophet.

The wait was over;
the father appeared, a bull of a man
dressed in green denim and sweat,
as the boy stared at the right hand
of the father, which held the razor strop,
once used by earlier generations

in an older country to hone
precision into a tailor's tools;
now it would serve to sharpen
a wayward boy's moral acumen.

With little enthusiasm
and less eye contact, the father
said, "Let's get this done."
The boy rolled obediently
onto his stomach and was stung
until all had been paid in full.

On those nights supper was served
and consumed in a forced silence
which the father chased down
with a few extra beers.
Later, as the family stared
at the black and white tv, the balance
seemed to return to their communal lives
as if some sacrifice had made things right.

Lou Ann Thompson   *Denton*

MUSKRAT LOVE

It was one of the taboos of divorce—going out with your ex. But the papers were all signed and filed over two years ago, each of them had had at least one transitional rebound affair, insurance companies had put a cap on the 50-minute therapy sessions, and their favorite musician, Willis Alan Ramsey, was making a rare performance in Fort Worth. Neither Sam nor Susan had ever missed one of his concerts, and it seemed the perfect opportunity for them to prove—to everyone, to each other, and to themselves—that they were completely over the marriage as well as the divorce, and they were mature, civil adults who just happened to have been married to each other.

The date was Sam's idea. He was going to be in Waco for a deposition, so he called Susan, who had moved back to Fort Worth shortly after he had moved in with Nat, and shortly before the divorce.

Susan's initial reaction was to say no when Sam suggested the reunion, "Kind of like Woodstock," he described it, as if dismissing the proposal lightly as more of an impersonal, historical/cultural obligation. But she had already asked everyone she knew to go with her, even asked some people she barely knew who worked at the paper, getting the same initial response from everyone—*"Who?"* That question was complicated by the difficulty of categorizing Ramsey's music, and whichever genre she focused on first always seemed to be the wrong one. If she described him as "country-ish" she found she was talking to someone who was "too intellectual" for country, whereas people who heard "folk" proudly informed her they had grown out of that phase. A few seemed willing to be persuaded at first, but their enthusiasm waned as soon as they asked, and they always did, "Well, has he done anything I might have heard of?"

Susan was prepared to answer, but she was just as well prepared to be rebuffed. "Well, now try to keep an open mind when I tell you," she warned, her voice sticking its foot in the door to the skeptic's narrow mind. "He wrote 'Muskrat Love.' But, believe me, it's completely different the way he does it." Although she tried to finish the second sentence before the first one had time to register, she knew her admonition would go unheard. It was deleted like all the words she tried to take back from her word processor, stored on some cosmic clipboard, waiting somewhere for the right moment to come back and incriminate her.

"You mean that Captain and Tenille song?"

Susan looked into eyes that nervously searched her for other previously unnoticed signs of bad taste. She began to think she knew how Jeffrey Dahmer felt when lunch was served.

"Yes," she confessed, frustrated, "but they *changed* it. It's not supposed to be so, so *cutesy*." She was tired of defending herself and Ramsey. Why did he have to write that song? But her invitation was already responded to with regrets, her reputation for aesthetic judgment already ruined. The few people who actually admitted to liking the song (interestingly, the last people she invited), were committed with family obligations and muttered something about how the kids would have probably enjoyed it and asked, didn't he write "Jeremiah Was a Bullfrog" too. Susan decided that no one born before Watergate wanted to go to concerts anymore, especially on a weeknight. She had resigned herself to going alone or missing a Ramsey concert for this first time in her life. She felt a twinge of stage three of the grief process when she realized that if she and Sam were still together she wouldn't have this problem. Moving on to stage four, she scolded herself for backsliding. And then, after all, Sam turns up, just in time. Sometimes, she thought, when you <u>need</u> a penny, even a bad one will do.

"The only trouble is," Sam said on the phone, "the distance. The firm isn't giving me a car down there since I'm staying at the airport hotel." Sam gulped in two minutes of air, as if he were diving into a familiar pond whose depth he wasn't sure he remembered.

"Oh, I can drive over and get you and take you back after the concert," offered Susan. She knew he was too cheap ever to rent a car with his own money—not a patent attorney who bought generic raisins and bran flakes separately to make his own raisin bran and save three bucks a year. No point in starting that argument again.

Sam tried not to sigh audibly into the mouthpiece. She hadn't changed that much, after all. Good old Suze, always quick to go out of her way for others. It was one of the things he had loved most about her. But nevertheless he protested, "That's too much trouble. It'll be so late when we get out, and you know how tired you get after ten." Sam started to feel comfortable displaying how he recalled his intimate knowledge of Susan's diurnal rhythms. "Besides, it must be about fifty miles."

"It's no trouble," Susan insisted. She, too, remembered her lines. And it was at least a hundred miles. "Besides, I stay up a lot later than I used to," she felt compelled to add. She entwined her fingers in the ecru phone cord which had coiled around the desk lamp.

"I guess I could get a hotel room," Sam offered. Susan could almost hear the computations of checkbook-balancing anxiety reach out and nudge her through the fiberoptics.

"That would be silly and a waste of money, since you have your room in Waco too. Besides, there is a big podiatrists' and chiropodists' convention here this week, and there isn't a room available in town. We've been covering it in the paper all week with these really stupid feature stories like 'What's A-Foot in Fort Worth This Week' and 'These Boots Weren't Made for Walkin'' so far. I can't believe I wasn't assigned those stories." Every time Sam's career moves required that Susan change jobs she basically had to start all over again. Despite her master's degrees in both journalism and political science, editors usually put her on lightweight assignments, like the fashion page she worked on for three years when they moved to Albuquerque. She learned more about colors and fabrics than any person should ever have to know.

"Well, I don't know anyone in Fort Worth anymore." Sam turned his face away from the phone and exhaled through his nose. His chest was tight, and he had to force his breath out in unsteady puffs. "Except you, of course."

"Listen, don't worry about it. It's not that big a deal. If I'm too tired, we'll just figure out something then. Okay?"

Sam thought he detected the musky scent of a nuance. "Okay," he agreed. "I'll call and reserve the tickets."

"I'll pick you up at 5:30. We can grab some dinner and get to the concert in plenty of time."

At 5:30, Sam opened the door into the room, which smelled like mold and carcinogens. "He forgot to ask for non-smoking," Susan thought. "Typical." Susan had always had to remember details like that when they traveled.

Both 5'10," Susan and Sam recalled simultaneously their many jokes about always seeing eye to eye and gave each other a noncommittal, timorous hug. Sam kissed her on the cheek. Something about the gesture seemed premeditated, Susan suspected.

Dinner and the drive were restrained, cordial—rather like a business lunch. Sitting across the table from this man felt unreal, and Susan wavered between trying to relax with her feelings of detachment and trying to analyze every detail. In many ways Sam seemed like a stranger, and Susan kept studying him for signs of the old and the new. She didn't recognize any of the clothes he was wearing—they actually matched and were made out of natural fabrics. She wondered who helped him pick them out, remembering that Nat had come and gone the same summer. The cord jeans were a bit wrinkled, but the color was still rich, a cocoa brown that was repeated in the background of the plaid flannel shirt. Thin, criss-cross lapis-blue lines were accentuated by his indigo knit tie. Talking to his profile in the car, Susan reminisced to herself about how she used to kiss the loose waves of mahogany hair that grew damp and turned to ebony, salty curls around his ears when he slept and how Sam would crinkle his nose without waking up.

Sam was amazed at how little Susan had changed, how easy it was to just pick up where they left off—before the bad part, that is. He congratulated himself on his maturity and sensitivity. He knew they'd always be friends, at least friends. Susan was dressed monochromatically, in taupe and mocha, he commented, reminding Susan of how she had taught him the names of so many colors she had learned while working on the paper.

Her eyes and her hair were still the color of Bit O'Honey, he added to himself.

When they got to the Will Rogers Auditorium, Susan couldn't believe the crowd, which bore a disturbing resemblance to her last high school reunion. Middle-aged. She overheard a couple of teenagers who had obviously been dragged along by their parents. "I bet we're the only ones here under thirty," snickered one with a pubescent complexion grotesquely enhanced by a tee shirt the color of lima beans. "Under fifty's more like it," reparteed the other.

Normally Susan would have been more annoyed, she thought, maybe even let Beavis here know she was still 39 for seven more months. But she was too distracted by the hundreds of people who not only knew who Willis Alan Ramsey was, but also even wanted to go see him and stay up late on a week-night. "Why don't I know any of *these* people?" she asked herself. Still, it was a fairly subdued crowd, a crowd that twenty-five years ago invented the rules of concert etiquette. And now they were complaining there was no decaf and opting for sparkling juice drinks, wearing Birkenstocks and stretch denim, still redolent of patchouli, and patiently explaining to their kids why it was "impor-tant" for them to be there. There would be no crowd surfing or moshing to-night.

Their seats were way in back, and before cursing Sam's frugality again, Susan reminded herself that they had ordered the tickets at the last minute. There was no warm-up band, and Ramsey simply walked on the stage and started to play without introduction. Susan thought that that's the way it should be. Dylan did that once. Honest, clean, to the point. Maybe he won't go for that fake, "spontaneous" encore stuff either. That was one of her generation's contributions to concerts she was not proud of. It was so dishon-est, so atypical of her generation, she thought, to pretend the show was over when everyone knew it wasn't.

Ramsey's voice still had that scratchy, smirky quality—it was never really a good voice—which was probably fortunate in a way, Susan reflected, since some months ago, she had been devastated to hear over-amplified instruments try to conceal one of cocaine's saddest victims, Stephen Stills' voice, once strong, clear and resonant in concert, now sounding as if it were actually coming from an original, badly scratched record. Ramsey knew how to please his audience too, and there was no excessive plugging of the new album, no attempt to persuade them to grow out of the good old days. He played everyone's favorites. Even the people who came for "Muskrat Love" were happy.

After playing an admirable two-and-a-half hours, Ramsey started to sing the raucous "Northeast Texas Women." Susan knew the concert was just about over, and she also knew her bladder couldn't survive the drive back. The ladies' room would be packed, of course, when the music was over. She tilted her head closer to Sam's. Their shoulders were already touching. "I'm going to the bathroom," she said. Her warm breath misted his ear and her tawny hair brushed across his neck. She smelled like a new love. "And I'm going to get the new c.d. You can never find his stuff in the stores. Do you want anything?"

"No," Sam answered, "but let me buy it for you."

He scooted forward in the metal seat and dug into his back jeans pocket with two fingers. Susan recognized the fuschia nylon and Velcro wallet he had carried for at least four years. Sam unwound the rubber band that held it to-gether and thumbed through the bills, lots of bills. "How much do you need?"

"I don't know." A spot of the muted concert light caressed a fleck in her candy eyes, and Susan giggled and said, "Why don't you just give me your wallet?" She lightly stroked the tip of her finger across his forearm. "Just like old times?" The hair on Sam's arm quivered. Susan could wink without twitching a lid.

"Hurry back," Sam requested, his voice softened like a Hershey Bar left on a carseat.

Susan tromped about twenty feet to the right, but seeing she was headed in the direction of the men's room, she turned back to go the other way. Inside, she bypassed the first row of stalls, and pushed the door of the very last one. She opened Sam's wallet. She found her picture, an old student I.D. Sam thought was sexy, in a hidden pocket behind the credit cards. She wondered if it was still there because he still cared or because he had just forgotten to take it out. She counted two hundred and sixty dollars. He still had his "Are You a Turtle?" membership card. And on the other side, in a small pouch for change, was a condom, with nonoxynyl-9, expiration date 7/98. Susan stared at the bottom hinge on the stall door, noting there were two mounting holes but only one screw. Evidently the screw had been missing for some time and was deemed unnecessary by the last painter, who sealed the hinge secure with a coat of new enamel. She remembered the old 1970s avocado paint she could see pushing its way through the flakes of newer, cheaper Santa Fe desert mauve. Her eyes were distracted by the stitching on her boots, her favorite boots.. She reached down and stroked the soft putty-colored suede that caressed her calf. These boots Susan sometimes thought of as her secret boots—so sexy they looked like they couldn't possibly have been designed to be worn by a woman with any place to go, but so comfortable she felt she could run a marathon in them. That image reminded Susan to get walking before the crowd started to spill out at once.

When the hunter-green Subaru was the first to pull up to the gate, the parking attendant asked, "Is the concert over?"

"No, just trying to get a head start," responded the driver, smiling. "Oh,"she fumbled around with things in the seat beside her. "I found this man's wallet. Will you turn it in to the Lost and Found for me?"

"Sure," said the guard, taking the bright pink bundle of nylon. "I *guess* we have something like that."

"Thanks," sang the driver. "Goodnight."

D. M. Heaberlin   *San Marcos*

ACROSS DAWN'S EDGE

We try to talk about

how across the edge of dawn

we see and hear

the wind and light and form of things.

We try to

but come out empty-mouthed

tongue-snubbed

while seeing the metamorphic light

bring,

in a blink,

new forms, new things newly lit

newly colored—

a green,

glowing

with violet and gold—

try and fail to find words

and settle for

the shapes and sounds

we have,

settle for this bird,

beating-

from the juniper grove,

suddenly,

bursting.

Michael Kearns   *Odessa*

DANCING IN WURZBURG

It was the Latin you said as your gaze glittered past me to the fourteenth century of the city map that had held you charged, tensed, the Latin unintelligible but profound which your dead friend Nelson who was a poet only in his soul would have loved, because he knew, you whispered, forgetting it was not a church, the trinity of poets and words and dance. Graced by the minuet of your hands set to no catholic cartographer's rhythm in that documents room of the city museum during a January storm, in that city and river under ice, I felt you dancing to other words than I had ever offered and because I remember your left hand stuck in your hip pocket and your right arm behind you, right hand grasping the left arm at the elbow, because I never sang your need I want to know whose incantation in what museum of emotions is plucking your strings today.

William McCarron   *Commerce*

FIXIN' TA LEAVE

"We're fixin' ta leave right now!" Maybelle Oates shouted up the stairwell. "Get the lead out and get down here, James Thomas! Grandma was never late for church and she won't be late for her own wake."

James Thomas, third and last of the Oates children, thudded down the stairs. "Twelve years old and yuh still don't know how to knot a tie," Maybelle muttered, grabbing the boy and whipping the faded silk around his neck. "And you, Herbert Oates, you know better than that!" She yanked the Bud longneck from her husband's fist. "Save yer drinkin' 'til after my mother's visitation."

Oates cussed and searched for the pick-up's keys in his pressed jeans. "My purse is on the chair. We'll take the Oldsmobile, not the pick-up. Keys are in the side pocket. Get them."

The late model Old 88 rested beside the old Ford pick-up in front of the garage. "The pick-up's gassed and ready, Maybelle—"

"But it ain't ready for my mother's wake, Herbert Oates. Besides, it's about as reliable as you are." Maybelle pointed to the battered pick-up. "Your pick-up is destined for the graveyard." The rusted Ford 150 seemed to sink like the lowering October sun. As if it were fixing to leave of its own accord for the junkyard.

* * *

Maybelle's daughter, Tammie, was handing a pen to each visitor lined up in front of the guestbook. "There's a crowd, mom. More than we expected," she whispered.

"Good girl," Maybelle said, patting her daughter's arm and entering the reception room where mourners were gathered near the open coffin. "She looks real peaceful like," Gloria Edom said to Maybelle. "She was a fighter. Not one to just fade away."

"One of a kind. That's for sure," Bobby Edom added.

Maybelle nodded. Ringlets of white hair framed the weather-beaten, angular face of the late Anna May Perkins. Maybelle had already ordered the duplicate headstone, which would rest beside her father's who had died in 1985. 'I am fixin' ta leave this world and join Elmo.' Maybelle remembered her mother's final words in the hospital.

Mourners filed by dutifully searching for consoling words. "I know. She was a wonderful, strong-willed woman," Maybelle found herself saying for the third time. Funeral sprays of carnations and roses seemed to bow at her words. "Thank you, Mrs. Fletcher," Maybelle nearly shouted into the hearing aid of the feedstore owner's wife. "We sure will take some time off now that the ordeal is almost over."

A half-hour later, as visitors began to dwindle, Maybelle felt a tug at the sleeve of her dress. It was Vera Sandusky, Maybelle's closest friend who owned Nails 'n' Stuff on the town square. Vera motioned for Maybelle to follow her.

Sequestered in a vacant side room, Vera spilled the beans. "You were right, Maybelle. They were in the Needles and Bark Motel over in Piney City. Mary Lou Hutton came out of the end unit and got in her Lincoln. Herbert slinked out of the same room about 15 minutes later. Lowered his John Deere cap as if that would hide his face. His pick-up was parked in a back alley."
Maybellle smacked her fist against the wall. "That's it! I'm fixin' ta leave him and his philanderin'!"

A few moments later there was a shuffling noise at the doorway. Herbert, Jr. stood, head hung, grasping his Stetson. "Mom," he stammered. "I know it's a bad time 'n all. But it's Doreen. She's in Crestview Manor again. Doctor says it's a bad breakdown. Doctor has her in the isolation unit."

Vera Sandusky sighed. "I was just fixing to take my leave," she said as Maybelle moved toward her eldest.

Herbert Jr.'s shirt pocket bore the words Editor, *Gilmarton Times-Dispatch*. The words were on every shirt he owned. He had inherited his mother's gift for writing. She hugged him. "Where's Timmie?" she inquired about Herbert Jr.'s only child.

"Tammie and Ray have him until after the funeral. I figured you and Dad had enough problems."

He stood back and stared down at his mother. "It's not Doreen's fault this time. The switch in medications didn't work." Maybelle muttered some words about doctors and their knowledge of prescription drugs for mental illness. "I'm fixin' ta leave for Crestview until she stabilizes," Herbert said, "but I'll be here for the funeral on Wednesday."

"Thank you, Herbert," Maybelle said. "May the Lord be with you."

* * *

The funeral home parking lot was nearly vacant when Maybelle exited the home's rear door. Tammie and Ray had already left in their new Dodge pick-up with James Thomas in tow. He had been thrilled when he learned he could play video games with his nephew, two years older than he.

Maybelle's quick green eyes caught her husband's figure near the Olds in the back of the lot. He was standing, hands dipped in the pockets at the back of his jeans, like he was reaching for his Copenhagen. Herbert Oates was sneaking furtive glances at a maroon Lincoln Town Car that had just driven up beside the carport where the hearse rested. Mary Lou Hutton was just emerging from the Lincoln and pressing her remote entry key. Maybelle watched as Mary Lou, looking like she was poured into her tight jeans, circled to the rear of her car and lifted the trunk. Mary Lou was reaching in for some plastic grocery sacks just as Maybelle passed her. Without a word, Maybelle marched toward a pile and returned with a single sharp-edged brick grasped in her right hand.

Fiercer than Nolan Ryan, Maybelle corked her arm and unleashed the brick at the front windshield. Pellets of shattered glass splattered over the hood and down the sides of the car.

"I'm fixin' ta leave more than a brick callin' card on your front seat, Mary Lou! If you ever, and I mean ever, come near my husband again! Ya hear!"

Mary Lou's sleek jaw dropped along with her grocery bags.

Having just emerged from his funeral home, silver-haired James Hutton stood transfixed, his usually placid demeanor only gradually registering what Maybelle had just said.

Cheryl Fries   *Austin*

LIFE ITSELF

I stare at the man in the moon and he looks back at me with empty indifference. I am just a speck, a collection of atoms so small I could disappear forever in the crater of his eye. The concrete exhales the day's scalding heat, thickening the night. Reflected on the police car in our driveway, even the moonlight looks hot.

Inside, two paunchy officers handle things. I don't watch, because I've seen it before. I read once that police officers dread these kinds of calls – domestic disturbance is their term – because they are so dangerously volatile. And yet, after they watch Cole drive away, they just shake their heads at me, get in their patrol car and do the same. We are left here alone, my mother and I, with only the moon to watch over us.

I go to my high school, walking from the classroom wing to the arts building in the afternoon's steaming heat. In the art room where I paint, the air is cool and we can hear the orchestra practicing down the hall. I watch Ms. Sylvester lean over Rod Carson's shoulder, murmuring encouragement. Ms. Syl, as we call her, wears big, vibrantly colored skirts and large, dancing earrings made of interesting materials: clicking shells one day, shiny oxidized metals the next. She is 31, just a few years younger than my mother.

Mr. Syl came to our class once, bringing lunch for his wife. Ms. Syl blushed when he kissed her cheek in front of us. They've been married two years. "No children – yet!" she told us on the first day of school. Mr. Syl is handsome and hip looking in shorts and hiking boots. He makes films. "Our home is a haven for creativity," Ms. Syl told us that first day, "And so is this classroom. You must create places that inspire your art. You are artists!" Ms. Syl has painted the classroom's walls, replacing the school's drab with a cool, watery lupine. She has softened the corners with potted palms, and brought in two aquariums swimming with brightly colored fish and a tabletop fountain that trickles water over a stone sculpture of the Muses. On the wall above the chalkboard Ms. Syl has hung a mint-colored banner with the phrase *Life Itself is Art!* painted in feathery purple strokes.

Being here is the best part of my day. I spread colors across my canvas: deep indigoes, seeping browns, pallid yellows—the colors of bruises. I watch the fish dart in the aquarium, startled by threats I can't know. Even in their confined tank, without predators, they are nervous, by instinct.

After school I walk the two blocks from the bus stop to our house. The sun hisses at me, spitting sweltering rays that bounce off the burning pavement, so hot it seems at any minute the whole world could ignite. I am overcome with violent hatred for it; I want to throw down my books, lift my head in raucous screams, stab it in the heart. But I am powerless beneath the sun's malevolence, so much bigger than I, so much older. I walk on alone, sweating in silence.

As I pass St. Michael's, I train my eyes ahead. We used to go to the Episcopal Church every Sunday, but when my father left he took our faith with him. Once, soon after, the priest came to visit, but my mother was too humiliated to face him. I guarded the doorway, told Father Rogers she was sick. He never came back.

It wasn't long before we moved into this rented house, so much smaller and older than the one I'd grown up in. But my mother tried, and, for a few weeks, before she met Cole, we actually had fun fixing it up. "It's like dressing up an old lady for a tea party," mom had said as she hung curtains she'd sewn from bridal-veil material she'd found on the remnant table at Wal-Mart. We planted zinnias from seed in the backyard and painted the kitchen a cheerful lemon-drop yellow. My mother gave me the spare room. "Your studio," she called it, and I set up my easels there – the only furniture in a room filled with boxes my mother refused to unpack.

I let myself in with the key I wear on a mauve ribbon around my neck and Randolph, my orange cat, runs to greet me. I carry him in one arm as I put away my schoolbooks and eat an apple. He purrs against my chest. There will not be a fight tonight. In the days after the police visit, Cole stays away and my mother comes straight home from work, swollen-eyed and tired, wearing dark glasses and long sleeves. She'll cook something easy and we'll read without talking at the table. After dinner she'll go to bed with ice packs on her spiraling bruises, their rings shooting out like the gasses of newborn planets, and I will do homework in front of the TV. The sky will darken around us and the moon will rise, smaller tonight. Randolph will sleep curled at my chest.

When my father calls we have clipped conversations, like strangers in line at a checkout counter. School is fine, I say. Randolph is fine. We don't mention mom or his new wife –his former secretary – or her daughter. They have moved far away, to the northeast where her parents live, so we talk about the differences in our weather. His is cool, rainy, the towering trees are beautiful. He does not invite me to visit and I am relieved. He has replaced us.

When I can't sleep, I've taken to stealing one of my mother's cigarettes and going out to sit on the concrete patio in the backyard, smoking and listening to the night bugs. I pretend I am Ms. Syl's daughter. We live in her house, which I furnish with beautiful things: hand-carved wooden tables, patchouli-scented candles, terra-cotta pots filled with cut flowers. We talk about art over dinner, Frieda Kahlo and Picasso's blue period, and eat gourmet pasta dishes Mr. Syl has cooked with wines and olive oils. On Saturdays we paint and watch foreign films on video and drink from solid mugs of coffee while it rains outside. The world is green and alive and cool air flows in through the opened windows. At night I sleep in a soft white bed with Randolph. The Syls come in to kiss me and whisper wishes for sweet dreams, then leave together, arms entwined. In this life, the moon glows like a welcome lantern though the clouds as I drift off, and the morning sun sings me gently awake.

I avoid the neighbors' eyes when I walk to the bus stop in the mornings.

They know I know they know. We are a bruise in their neighborhood, attracters of squealing tires, angry screams, police cars at night. We are all embarrassed at our powerlessness and they avoid our contagion. I am tense this morning after my mother's bright announcement: *I'll be late tonight. Cole and I are having dinner.* I sneer visibly at Julie Grayson and her two silly cheerleader friends as they giggle on the bus. I don't care when I hear them whisper *she's such a bitch* as I pass.

In history class I have even less patience than usual with the buffoon coach who passes himself off as a teacher. He is stupid and brawny, bulging from his polyester coaching uniform. He slaps Derek Roberts on the back and I see his hand slamming against his wife, knocking her across the room, where she lands against a table and breaks the sculpted cat her daughter made in fourth grade. She cries out and slumps to the floor, gathering broken shards in her bleeding hands, and he pounces like a shark, pulls her by the hair, screams *you slut.* I am there, dressed in the uniform of a policewoman, gun poised. He looks at me and I shoot him through the heart.

Ms. Syl compliments my painting to the class. "Audrey's use of color is superb. The tones of night are captured beautifully. The work screams at us initially, but is balanced by the peaceful full moon and the ringed planets that rise in her sky. It seems to suggest a continuity in the universe on which we can all rely. You are an artist, Audrey!"

Later, I stare at the painting. I have brought it home and put it on the easel in my studio room. I study the moon I have painted, searching vainly for the peace Ms. Syl saw. But he looks back at me contemptuously – *fooled 'em all, haven't we?* Outside I hear a squeal of tires, the screech of brakes in front of my house, the argument rising as the earth spins, growing fuller in the night.

I close the door to the room and pick up my paintbrush. The voices outside build in the darkness. Through the window I see the new moon, a slivering sneer of light. I watch it for a minute. Then I dip my brush into the paint.

Alyce M. Guynn   *Austin*

A SHINER FOR ROSE

Rita was driving blind. Sheets of rain spread across the windshield faster than the wiper blades could push them aside. The sky was black—falling-in black. Traffic, thick. Just as a diesel passed on her left, splashing a sea-sized wave against her Datsun, the wipers stopped. She flicked the switch on and off. Nothing. Her leg began trembling, then went into a jerk. The palms of her hands got so clammy she could hardly hold the wheel. "I'm in God's hands," she said, feeling totally out of control. Just then the Datsun swerved off the road, veering down a twenty foot embankment. She was floating.

When she surfaced her leg was still twitching, hands still sweaty.

Rita reached for the bedside lamp and sat up to light a cigarette. She was unnerved by the dream. Driving blind. Out of control. That was her life.

In the kitchen she heated water for a cup of chamomile tea. She moved quietly, careful not to clank the dishes, lest she wake Henry. She'd stopped telling him her dreams a long time ago.

Sitting at the table, Rita hoarded the warmth of the cup, letting the steam surround her nose and mouth. She reflected on the simple pleasures of her kitchen table. She lit a candle, wrapped her flannel nightgown around her knees, drew her feet up and hooked them in the hem. She felt swaddled. She drank the tea. Sedated, she returned to bed.

By the time the alarm went off, the nightmare had been buried intoRita's subconscious. She and Henry drank their usual two cups of coffee while passing sections of the newspaper back and forth. They didn't say much. It was a work day, so both moved through the morning bathroom routines quickly and left for their respective jobs.

Rita didn't usually take the upper deck of IH35, but this morning she was running a little late. A constant succession of cars sped by in the outer lanes, ignoring the 55-mile speed limit.

She leaned over to turn on the radio. Not a sound. Something uneasy began to stir in Rita, but she couldn't identify it. Not until the drops began to splatter the windshield.

Rita felt her heart enlarge. It throbbed heavy as she saw the black of the sky ahead of her. The dream tapped her on the shoulder.

Terrified, she tried! the radio again. Nothing. She waited to test the wipers. The rain was still identifiable drops.

Not for long. Suddenly, everything shifted gears, and Rita could only see a blur of watery windshield. Now she reached for the wiper switch. Nothing. Her leg started trembling as she reached again for the switch. Her hands went slippery cold. "I'm in God's hands," Rita remembered.

This time God took better care of her and somehow she exited the freeway. She hadn't collided with other cars or slipped off an embankment.

By the time she arrived at work, Rita was so relieved to be alive she turned loose of the fear. Soon the regularity of her work routine dulled the memory of this morning's brush with death and the shuddering aspects of the prophetic dream. Life got back into perspective by coffee break.

Still, Rita was ecstatic to see the sun at quitting time. She scouted the sky for any signs of sneaky clouds. There weren't any. Out of habit Rita reached for the radio. The Oakridge Boys blared out "You're always in my heart and often on my mind." Startled, Rita looked back up at the cloudless sky. She felt for the wiper switch and cringed as the blades squeaked across the dry glass.

Something to be learned here. But she was too worn out to delve into it.

At home she wriggled out of her uncomfortable work clothes and binding shoes. When she finally got down to the panty hose, her whole body took a deep breath, allowing air into her pores for the first time all day. She was glad she and Henry weren't seeing each other tonight. She needed space.

Even though Rita w! as the one who often pushed for marriage, the truth was she enjoyed her solitude at times. This was one of them. The day had stretched her thin.

A hot bath would pull her back in. She put on the tea kettle and ran the bath water. Rita liked to drink tea in the bathtub. Well, anywhere, really. But the tea, along with incense and candle, were part of her bath therapy.

She laid her head back on the end of the tub and watched her toes. Her breathing slowed and her chest heaved a sigh of relaxation. Then she realized she'd forgotten to remove the ring. She took it off and set it on the toilet top, making a mental note so she would remember where she'd left it.

Rita loved that ring. It had been Henry's concession. Formal marriage: no. But a ring, something just between the two them—he could go that far. It was an eternity ring. Twenty-one rubies in a channel lock setting. Eternity he could live with; marriage vows, he could not.

Rita was happy with the ring. She was pretty happy with Henry.

But how Rita relished these moments of leisure and solitude. She splashed water on her breasts and wished she could quiet the conflict inside her. Tiny lips sucking on her tits. Singing lullabies in a darkened room. Yeah, she wanted that some of the time. But mostly, like in moments such as these, she just enjoyed being alone. She cherished the control she had over her time. A husband and children would make demands. They would be so draining. Rita felt immediately guilty for not whole heartedly wanting what she had been brought up to believe was the perfect dream.

She liked the unwed imperfection of her relationship with Henry. Seeing him frequently, but by appointment, satisfied her but never satiated her. He locked his secrets away from her, never revealing his soulful thoughts or feelings. It annoyed her greatly, but it kept her coming back for more. He often seemed unattentive and distracted a lot, whetting her curiosity while she sank into an undefinable insecurity. Something was always coming up short between the two of them. Everything was never all right.

The ring was like that. To Rita it had become a symbol of the imperfection between them. The deep carmine shine of those perfect rubies, set in that silly white gold. Rita hated white gold. She always had, even as a child. An imitation of platinum, not proud pure gold in its own right. The ring was missing something. She and Henry were missing something.

Well, tonight she didn't have to worry with it. She was alive and happy. After her bath, Rita curled up in her pink satin down comforter and drank Almond Sunset tea while she wrote letters and talked to her women friends on the telephone.

Drifting into her dream, Rita saw the woman Rose. The name seemed incongruent. Sleek and sensuous, she looked more like a Stella. The woman was wearing a shiny black dress that hit her knees. Rose was smoking imported, long brown cigarettes and drinking Shiner beer. Another inconsistency. Dream license. Henry in the picture. Anxiety. Blurred movement, music. In the final frame, Rose was draped around Henry as they danced in an intimate embrace.

Rita woke with a snap. Sharply, she pulled herself into reality. She was shaking. Not this again. She thought they had this question settled. The ring had symbolized the end to unfaithfulness. It was, after all, a dream, not a confession. Still, her guts tightened and her eyes narrowed. Sitting up for a cigarette, she reached for the phone. This time she would break her rule about not sharing dreams with Henry. She needed consoling; he wouldn't be angry at her waking him. Her fingers automatically pushed the right buttons. On the sixth ring, Rita stubbed out the cigarette and immediately lit another. She looked at the clock: one a.m. Henry wasn't home. She dropped the receiver on the hook, but absent-mindedly held onto it.

An hour later she was still chain smoking and pushing buttons. Nothing changed. No answer. Every act of infidelity—real and imagined—of the last four years moved across the movie screen of Rita's mind.

Sleep would not return. No amount of chamomile tea and candles could obliterate the dream. Rita agitated until four a.m., when finally she escaped into sleep.

At work the next day she was so obsessed she couldn't concentrate. Henry called to confirm their Friday night dinner plans.

"I can't stay on the phone long; I have a lot of work," she said, cutting the conversation short.

"Okay, I'll just see you tonight about seven."

There was a smugness in his voice. She was sure of it. Well, she couldn't let all of this interfere with her work too much. She hated for her emotions to interrupt her work day. Somehow she kept up appearances of productivity, and left a little before five o'clock.

When she started the ignition and reached for the radio, silence saluted her. Not this again. She opened the door and slammed it real hard. Radio on. Short circuit. Something to be learned here, but she didn't want to fool with it.

She still wasn't sure how to deal with Henry and the subject of infidelity. A direct confrontation wouldn't work. It never did. Henry had the silver tongue of a trial lawyer. She could never compete in their serious discussions. Actions not words. Henry must be screwing around. Why else would he be so opposed to marriage? Still, she was looking forward to seeing him for their regular Friday night. Usually, no matter how mad she was, seeing Henry's dancing blue eyes always watered down her anger. Feeling his body press against hers always fogged over her clarity.

Tonight she would have to fight against that. Something had to be settled once and for all.

Henry was happy at the thought of seeing Rita tonight. Yesterday's trial had been rough on him, had left him wound tight. Being with Rita usually made him forget the tensions and pressures of his law practice. In addition to his usual worries, the neighbors had wakened him at midnight, asking him to drive them to the emergency clinic. The husband had cut his thumb in his workshop, and the wife couldn't handle the cut, the car, the kids, and the clinic without help. So, Henry's sleep had been interrupted several hours in a Samaritan venture into the night.

He would leave all that behind. Henry didn't like to bring petty details into his moments with Rita. Being with her could work like a two-hour massage, a movie set in a foreign land. Escape from reality.

She had added so much to his life. Henry had never known a woman like Rita. But he couldn't take her intensity 24 hours a day, seven days a week. He needed breaks in between. Often Henry wished Rita could bring herself to read detective novels or serve meatloaf, or anything that hinted at the ordinary.

She was always pondering the condition of the universe, probing his feelings until he felt raw. Sometimes she clawed and scratched at the edges of his soul as though she wanted to climb inside. Probably, Henry conceded, she just wanted to get a good look at it. Still, he didn't like it. Rita clung to every nuance and moved in constant subtleties and shades of difference.

Rita looked at life by candlelight. She insisted they eat in the shadowy, subdued flicker of the candle she set on the kitchen table in perpetual ritual. She even kept one in the bathroom. Next to the kitchen candle Rita set a bud vase. Empty, it invited her favorite flower: the yellow rose. She liked dining to a single yellow rose by candle. Over the years Henry had fallen into the habit of bringing her one on Friday nights.

Tonight was no different. Henry carefully gathered the green tissue paper as he slid from behind the wheel. He wondered which of Rita's long, flowing at-home gowns she would wear this evening. Something magenta or burgundy, he projected. She seemed to change her moods by changing clothes and colors.

Rita puzzled Henry. Her world was a bit too other to suit him. Sometimes he longed to sit beside her drinking a six pack, watching football on T.V. No chance for that. Henry had accepted it. But at least her insane jealousy had subsided since he'd given her the ruby ring.

At least that was the way it had been for several months.

Henry greeted Rita with the rose. She retreated from the hello hug. Henry had been right about the color burgundy. Rita swirled around in the folds of her gauze gown and handed Henry the empty bud vase while she turned to stir the cream of leek soup.

He filled the vase with water, trimmed the stem of the rose, and ceremoniously set it next to tonight's candle.

The table was set with Rita's usual simplicity. Henry looked at his placemat and white porcelain dish. It held a tiny satin pillow cradling the ruby ring.

Oh-oh, Rita's mad. He had no idea why. But then, he seldom knew her mind. Inscrutable was the word he often used to describe her.

Well, the scene was too orchestrated to ignore.

"What's this doing here?"

"I don't want it. It doesn't mean anything." She stirred the soup.

"Doesn't mean anything?"

"Take it back and keep it 'til you're ready to put in on my finger inside a church. And what's more: I want a baby."

Henry wanted to hit her.

"Not this again. I can't take it tonight, Rita. It's been a hard week. Lighten up, please. Let's have a pleasant dinner. I was looking forward to it."

Rita stirred the soup. She was fighting back tears. "Well, I can't take not talking about it. So where does that leave us?" Rita said.

"I don't know where it leaves you, but it leaves me out. I'm leaving. I'll call you tomorrow." Henry slammed the door.

Rita slid down to the kitchen floor with her back to the stove and sobbed into burgundy gauze. She reached up behind her and turned off the soup. Shadows of the candle played across the single yellow rose.

She could hear the dimming sound of Henry's engine as it topped the hill and rounded the corner.

Henry drove wrecklessly with no specific direction.

"Goddamn her eyes," he said out loud.

Rita had a way of throwing a dash of vinegar on everything that was potentially sweet. And always when he least expected it. For the life of him, Henry couldn't figure that woman out. This was a lot of the attraction, and he knew it. But he was too wound tight to deal with her tonight. He had hoped for something intimate and not intense. Fat chance.

Maybe he should agree to marriage. But the minute the thought came up, Henry stomped it in the ground. Rita didn't want him. Not in that kind of way. She didn't even really know who he was.

Rita thought if a little bit was good, a whole lot should be better. Henry knew different. She ought to. Rita cooked with spices. Marry her? That would be the quickest way to lose her. Henry didn't really want to lose Rita, although right now that didn't seem like such a bad idea. She had most likely given him another sleepless night.

Without thinking, Henry turned off Lake Austin Boulevard into Deep Eddy Cabaret. A couple of beers would calm him down. Maybe he'd call her after he'd had time to get over being so angry.

He had his two beers and realized that he hadn't even noticed when the bar stool next to him stopped being empty. She was pulling a long cigarette from her purse.

”Can I get a light?” she asked.

”Sure.”

The flicker of Henry's lighter sent a shimmer across the woman's face, and she smiled sensuously into his eyes.

”Do you come here often?” He pocketed the lighter.

”No, just to hear the band. I like to dance to their music.” Her shoulders moved to the anticipated rhythm.

”I haven't danced in a long time. But I just might tonight. What's your name? Can I buy you a beer?”

She nodded. “Rose.”

Henry looked on the label of her bottle and called to the bartender, ”A Shiner for Rose.”

Teresa Acosta   *Austin*

I'M AFRAID THAT IT'S TOO LATE TO BE ON THE SIDE OF THE FISH

A friend shows me a cheap pix of a man and a fish
from a weekend trip.
You know the rest. A trophy story ensues
in which said gigantic fish will be mounted
and mantled or put in some other non-fishy
landlocked showcase.

The story will, no doubt, list
the dangers el pescador faced:
the boat almost capsizing, the fish fighting
all the while, 'til even past the end
when it thrashed through its last moments.
My friend recalls this with a mixture of dismay
and acceptance of what must be
when a fish encounters one of us.

From his stuffed, non-fishy, landlocked showcase
the fish's eyes are frozen on me as I pass by.
He knows that mouthing platitudes
could not save him nor will they ever save
anything I say I love.

No matter how such I protest,
how much I insist that
I wanted him:
to live, to grow fat, to die of old age.

Jerry Bradley   *Beaumont*

EARSHOT

The contrail eddies and bends its back,
then opens its fist and spiders
into a noiseless dot. The missile
we never saw thrusts toward Utah,
its dummy warhead punching holes
in blue September's clouds. Tracing its climb
with a finger, we watch the sky open,
then clot close behind.
               That day we hiked
the canyon wash, your dog spooked rabbits,
dozens, from their pm shade. The next rain
erased her tracks and ours.
              What we want,
we say, is a warning shot, thunder beating light
down the arroyo in time for us to hear what comes.

But what hides best is sound—the crack of the bullet
is never first to reach the heart. Like the picture tube
dissolving in the quicksand of itself, it goes deaf
before blind.
              Dumb instrument, the tongue's
too subtle a thing; it means to report
what another needs to hear but always arrives late,
just as something lovely has gone out of sight,
leaving it to stammer in the rinsing rain,
you were the most wonderful person in the world.

Beverly Forsyth   *Odessa*

THE KNOCK

(for P.)

Come in.
I've been waiting.
I had given up,
gotten tired, and   .
shut that door
when your knock woke me
from a sleep from which
I could barely move.
But the door reverberated long
And with such longing
My limbs compelled me to move.
Groggy, heavy with sleep
I stumbled to the door.
Many times before, I had heard a knock
and rushed to answer it
with tightened breath, pulse racing.
When I got there,
Calling shadows teased and danced along my porch.
Night noises made by night things bumping against the outside wall.
It had happened so many times before
that I no longer roused.
Or if I did, I peeked outside my window
and returned to bed, imprinted warm with my body.
And then you knocked . . .
and knocked . . .
and knocked again . . . .
Come in.
Lie beside me.
I've been waiting.

Sybil Pittman Estess   *Houston*

THERE ARE NO TIGERS

"There are no tigers in the back yard; she is
lying," he said to her mother about her when
she was three. Her father, who had a hard time

with flowers, all things to be grown, including
kids. He had come up on a farm earlier.
How he hated grass, even--having to mow it. . . .

But the green things he despised most were
wiles. Imagination fits in her even when
she was that tiny tot . . . with lots of space,

endless energy to see those big beasts,
growling. She was proud, too, when he hit
her for fibbing or racing by his mowing

machine that never cut down her tiny
vow not to tell him more tales. Now
she's near sixty. Those stripe-filled faces

petition her to play. Like haunts, they follow
for fun. She watches well, does not tell him
all wild things he could not let me see or say.

Alan Lee Birkelbach   *Plano*

MOVING THE PERUVIAN MUMMIES

Into the cliff dwellings the archeologists climbed like arthritic monkeys.
They stirred the pot shards, dissembled old shawls, misinterpreted hieroglyphs.
They came with their questioning meters and their steaming, humid bodies.
They came, already tasting the heady, air-conditioned endorphins that would
come to their tongues when they stood in the crush outside the temperature-
controlled glass cases where the mummies would be moved. They took the
mummies that had presided unruffled in these caves for centuries. They wrapped
them like papooses and layered them with rags to catch each and every decay-
ing flake as the omnivorous air, held so long at bay, finally began to gnaw. And
when all the taut-skin bundles had been boxed then those archeologists looked
at each other with somehow different eyes, knowing they had lost their pillag-
ing virginity, and they justified it by saying, over and over, how nothing can
remain intact.

Leslie Stanley-Stevens   *Stephenville*

NOBODY'S FAULT:

Genesis 3:1-6 (Revised Stanley perVersion)

One day Eve needed someone to talk to, but Adam was busy with his man's work—naming things. Fortunately, she met a serpent, Pat, who was quite a good conversationalist and before they knew it, it was time for lunch.

"Do you want some grapes?" asked Eve (always the perfect hostess).

"No, I can't reach them and besides, I think they're sour. But I brought some bananas. Would you like a bite?"

"Gee, I appreciate your offer" (never wanting to offend) "but God told us not to eat bananas."

"Oh, I can't imagine that," retorted Pat. "Bananas are the perfect happy food—High in potassium, you know. Also, there's a great view of our neighbor's garden from the top of the banana tree."

"Neighbor? Who is my neighbor?"

"Neighbors are people who fall into ditches. You're supposed to love them."

Pat didn't realize that God had made bananas the forbidden fruit. God told Pat not to eat pomegranates. (It gets complicated here, but it has to do with serpent digestion.) So when Pat explained that it was pomegranates that were forbidden, Eve doubted herself and bit into the banana.

Adam came by during a coffee break and picked up a banana without even asking what it was. Since Adam was in charge of naming things, it never occurred to him that what he was eating could be a banana.

He had named it "apple."

Jerry Craven   *Canyon*

PEPPER CANDY

"You can't invite your friends." Dad shook his head. "I'll explain it when we drive to San Tomé this evening. You ride up front with me and your mother, and we'll show you how the camp is laid out."

"He's seen how the American camp is laid out," Carl said.

"Yes. But he never knew why. Tonight he learns why."

That evening as the sun neared the horizon, Dad drove us out of the village, across the El Tigre River and toward San Tomé. My sister and brother rode in the back of the pickup; I sat up front with Mom and Dad. At North Camp we bumped across a cattle guard at a gate that was always open. "What did you notice about the gate, Jerry?" Dad asked.

"It was open."

"Good. Look ahead at the houses on the right. What do you notice about them?"

I sat on the edge of the seat and inspected the row of houses. "They're white. They have tin roofs."

"Corrugated zinc. Yes. What else?"

"They're big. Bigger than the mud-and-thatch houses in our village." I looked at Dad to see if I was getting it right.

He nodded. "Who lives in those houses?"

"Venezuelans. Some of them came from our village."

Dad drove to a gate in the fence and stopped while one of the men from the guard house came out to look at us. He waved us through. "What's different about that gate?"

"It has a guard."

"Why did he let us through?"

"He lets everyone through."

"No, son. He does not. He let us through because we're white."

"I'm not white. I'm brown from the sun."

Mom shook her head. "He means you're not a native."

"His job is to keep the natives out of South Camp," Dad said.

"I've seen natives over here."

"True. They come in during the day to work. They don't come in at night. Where are the bigger houses of South Camp?"

"They get bigger as we go that way." I pointed.

"Yes. Away from North Camp and toward the clubhouse where they show the movies on Saturday. Toward *Jefe* hill. Houses around the hill are the biggest ones. The men who live in these houses are the most important people in the oil company. The hill wasn't a hill until the dirt movers made it. The idea is the most important man lives on the highest spot in the camp. Down the hill are men who are important, so they have big houses, but smaller than the one on top. The houses get smaller all the way to where?"

"To the fence at North Camp." I slid down in the seat.

"And on the other side of the fence? Smaller houses for natives."

"Why can't they come to the movie? Why can't they take their kids and drive through that gate and go into the clubhouse to get popcorn then go out on the back lawn to see the movie like everyone else?"

"You tell me why, Jerry." Dad's voice was almost a whisper.

I wouldn't answer. We rode on toward the clubhouse on the side of *Jefe* Hill. I stayed hunkered down on the seat, looking up at the mango trees, at the way the leaves looked dark against the last streaks of daylight. If I sat up I knew I would see zinnias and rose bushes in the yards, tiny pepper plants with fiery red fruit on them ("hotter than blue blazes," Dad had once said about the ornamental peppers), grass, hedges of oleander, and big houses of important men living near the hill that wasn't a hill before the dirt movers came in.

As he parked near the clubhouse, Dad said, "So you see, son, even if we brought your friends from the village, the guards at the gate stop us. If we sneaked them past the guards, people here in San Tomé would make us take them away. Nobody wants natives to come into South Camp after dark."

The parking lot was a mess of shadows thrown in several directions by a few street lamps. I got out of the pickup feeling dispirited about seeing a movie Ramón and Sylvia were not allowed to see because they were *natives*, people who couldn't get through the South Camp gate because they were too brown and because they lived in the village in tiny houses.

"Come on," Carl called to me.

I joined him on the sidewalk. Oleanders loomed tall and dark, and ahead I could see in the yellow lights of the clubhouse people milling around the popcorn counter. A girl with pretty blond hair stood in the center of the room, and I remembered her name was Peggy. Beside her stood a big guy the kids called Ed, who was Peggy's brother.

Not long after Carl and I got popcorn, everybody went out back to a grassy place with metal chairs set in front of the movie screen. The projector had already begun to sputter, and among the odors of popcorn and crushed grass I could smell odd fumes from the projector, a smell Carl said came from hot film. Adults chose the seats back from the screen. Carl and I found a place on the grass off to one side. That way if the movie turned out bad, we could sneak into the dark and go to the room with the popcorn machine.

People laughed at the cartoon, but I didn't see much funny about it. A big stupid cat kept trying to find ways to catch a smart little mouse, but the cat didn't have a chance. The mouse came up with ways to burn the cat's whiskers off or skin him or smash him so flat that he walked around for a few steps like a sheet of paper with feet. I was glad when the movie came on.

It didn't look so promising either because it was about a tall skinny guy who kept dancing with a pretty woman. Carl tugged at my shirt to let me know he had seen enough just when the skinny guy took the pretty woman into his arms and kissed her.

They had to turn their faces sideways so they wouldn't bump noses, and they pressed their lips together. Carl tugged at my shirt again but I wanted to watch them kiss. They seemed to think the kiss was the grandest thing anyone could do. "Come on," Carl whispered like he was talking to a dolt.

I got up and backed away from the screen, watching the kiss, and tripped on someone's leg. When I hit the ground I was almost nose-to-nose with Peggy, who sat on the grass, and for a crazy moment I thought she wanted me to turn my head so our noses wouldn't bump and kiss her. I scrambled away toward Carl.

Inside the clubhouse Carl and I picked through the unpopped kernels of corn in the popper when Peggy came in. "If you want a treat, I'll give you one," she said in a sweet voice. She moved close to me, and I looked with awe at her silky hair and bangs, at the scattering of freckles on her cheeks. She laughed. "Open your mouth and close your eyes, and I'll put a wonderful piece of candy in your mouth."

"Don't do it," Carl warned.

"You shut up," Ed said from the doorway.

But I knew Carl was wrong to be alarmed. I closed my eyes.

"Open wider." She put something in my mouth. "Now bite down. Hard."

I pushed her treat to the back of my mouth and bit down. It was like biting into a red-hot ember. I spat out the ember, noting with a part of me that I had just spat an ornamental pepper onto the front of Peggy's dress, but the image seemed irrelevant. My mouth hurt like no pain I had ever known. There were some odd noises in the room, but I couldn't identify them. The only thing that seemed to exist with crystal clarity was the burning of my gums and tongue.

Carl shoved Peggy aside and pulled me toward the concession counter. "Quick," he said, "wash out your mouth with this." He handed me a bottle. I took a swig, but the liquid made the burning worse. I spewed it onto the floor.

"That's awful!" Peggy said, laughing.

Laughter, I thought. That's the odd sound. Laughter.

"You're going to have to clean that mess up," Ed said. He, too, was laughing.

"Yeah," another boy said. "And pay for that Coke."

"*Vamos*," Carl said, taking my arm. "*Todos aquí son cabrones.*" The people here are goats. But why was he speaking Spanish, I wondered, even as I followed.

"Listen," Ed said. "They've gone native."

"Get out of the way." Carl pushed Ed aside and pulled me out the front door. Then he switched to Spanish again and told me he had seen a garden hose out front.

A group of kids followed us and watched Carl get the hose going. I ran the stream of water into my mouth, and it seemed to help some.

"Are you going to let that *native* boy push you like that, Ed?" Peggy said.

"Talk English," one of the boys demanded.

"Guards don't let natives through the gate," I tried to say, but the words came out a blurred gurgle.

Ed snatched the hose from me and swung it at my head. I ducked. The hose whistled over my head and hit Carl. He fell into some oleander bushes. At that moment, a baldheaded man came out of the clubhouse. "What are you kids doing with that hose?" he demanded.

"Just playing." Ed dropped the hose.

"You kids get back to the movie or else go into the clubhouse."

"How is your mouth?" Carl asked, still in Spanish.

"Native boy, native boy." Peggy chanted the words with a sneer on her face. "Native boy has a cut ear, don't you, native boy?"

Carl had a drop of blood clinging to his earlobe, though he seemed unaware of it. He picked up the hose.

"You boys leave that water alone, now."

"It's all right," I told Carl in English.

"Let's go to the pickup," Carl said.

"We'll be back," Ed said in a mean whisper. He and Peggy and a couple of other kids went into the clubhouse.

"My mouth hurts."

"I know. Those peppers are bad. Come on, now. I think there might be some water in Dad's Gott can in the pickup."

When we climbed into the back of the pickup, Carl pulled the top off of the water can, held it under the spout, and drew some water. "Wash your mouth out with this. Just swish it around on the burn and spit it out. And give me your Barlow."

I swished and spat as he instructed, aiming the water over the side of the truck, then gave him my pocket knife.

Carl hopped out of the pickup. "Those mean kids are coming back, and I'm going to be ready for them."

"Don't hurt Peggy. She made a mistake when she put that pepper in my mouth. She meant to give me a piece of candy." I spat and took another mouth-ful of water.

"That's dumb." He vanished into the oleander bushes at the edge of the parking lot. When he returned, he carried a long branch and was busy whack-ing the leaves from it.

"Dad said." I took another swig and spat. "Oleanders are poison."

"I know. But I don't plan to eat it." The branch he stripped looked straight enough to be a small spear or an arrow. "Here they come. Remember to talk only Spanish. Some of these idiot kids have lived in Venezuela as long as we have, and they don't know a word of Spanish."

"Peggy isn't an idiot."

Ed and two boys stood under the streetlight closest to our pickup. Carl held the oleander arrow in the shadows behind him. "Just stay in the pickup," he said in Spanish.

"Listen, Ralph. I told you he had gone native," Ed said.

"Yeah," Ralph said. "Hey native boy. Are you going to come to my house to cut the lawn? Is your mama going to come clean our house and wash my underwear?" The three boys laughed.

"If you want," Carl told me in Spanish, "spit some water on them."

I took a swig and spewed it on Ed and the other two guys.

"Crap!" Ed said. "I'll beat the snot out of you for that." He started for the side of the pickup.

Carl whipped the oleander branch around, making it whistle in the air. He hit Ed's shoulder. Ed yelped and scrambled away. Carl made the oleander whistle again and Ralph made a funny whimpering sound. When the oleander whistled again, the boys were out of range. "Come on back," Carl said. "If you stand over here and open your mouths and close your eyes, I'll give you a treat." The oleander whistled a couple of times, and the boys vanished into the clubhouse.

"You still want to bring Ramón and Sylvia into South Camp to see a movie?" Carl asked. "Would you want to introduce them to Peggy and Ed?"

I took another mouthful of water and spat it on the parking lot. "It was a mistake," I said. "Peggy made a mistake." I started to add that she had wanted me to kiss her, but decided it best not to say anything else.

Cyra S. Dumitru   *San Antonio*

MARCH: CIBOLO CREEK, BOERNE

Following months and months of scant rain, the day comes
when the creek can barely stir, loses its sense of current,
and rests holding its breath like a thin stone. Slowly
there grows upon the stillness a mask of algae, duckweed
that clings to the stalled surface like the skin of a sleeping
lizard, and you dream for a moment that you could tiptoe
across its great back to touch tree shadows leaning textured
as real bark. Then reason prevails. Instead you toss a stone
into the green, listen as the thropping carves a dark opening,
allowing you to glimpse memories of flow and of what once
surged downstream. Suddenly the green heals itself.
You are driven to wound once more, to see whether the river
can seam itself whole again, and again and endlessly again.

Barbara Fryrear   *Irving*

THE GUY NEXT DOOR

I want to be a good neighbor. I've invited him for coffee as a thank-you for helping me with the bird bath. He was sitting on his front step when I drove up with this big concrete thing hanging out of the bungie-strapped trunk of my Toyota. So here he is on my patio, sipping coffee from my carafe, laced with whiskey from his silver hip flask. This makes me uneasy.

I've not had much experience with men of the world. My husband was a good man with simple ambitions, whereas this guy from next door should be downing rum in a bar in Havana. With those Hemingway looks, he should be inventing stories that the world is waiting for on his old Underwood. Instead, he's telling me one of them now.

He says Ruthie left last night to take care of a sick aunt in Little Rock. He must know that their argument was so loud I couldn't help but hear her yelling and slamming out of the house. He says she lost her ring in the pool, and he can't wait to show her that he's dived down and found it. He holds out his thick right hand to show me the diamond-studded gold band on his pinkie.

While his hand is still out, he sort of flashes the fat gold bracelet on his hairy wrist. He guesses I want to know where that came from, so he lowers his voice and leans closer.

He hints he was with "The Company," recruited right out of the Air Force because of his outstanding record and made bodyguard to the president of El Salvador, or Equador. Hard to make out which. He's whispering.

He's into his fourth cup, only he skips the coffee this time, and he starts to pull up his shirttail to show me the machete scar he collected in the line of duty. El Presidente was so grateful–for what, he doesn't say–so grateful that he presented this guy with that gold bracelet.

That's when I decide the birds must be real thirsty. I go for the hose with him so close behind me I can smell the coffee. I figure the water might make a weapon somehow. I've seen him go off from time to time in some sort of uniform, or part of one–a shirt with a flag on the sleeve and crisp white pants and shoes and a straw hat. Is he trained to kill? Does he get crazy violent when he drinks? I have a fleeting fear that with Ruthie gone, he may turn into a sex maniac. Nah. He'd go for a younger, skinnier woman.

"Ruthie's left me," he sobs.

Oh, lord. That's worse than what I feared. He snakes a handkerchief from his hip pocket and blows his nose. Says he spent all night after she left writing poems he knows will melt her heart if she'll only read them.

So he is a writer, I think, not bothering to wonder if the poems are any good. I like a macho man if he's got the soul of a poet. I sit down again. Bad idea.

He tenses up, remembering their argument I guess. Then he hits the glass table so hard I'm afraid it will crack. I ask him where he was born. Reduce him to a baby, I'm thinking, or at most a small boy. I can handle a small boy. Then I can ease him toward home by the side gate.

He was born in the Air Force, he says, and before that doesn't matter. First folks that ever cared for him. Taught him to be a man. Saddest day of his life was when he had to leave the Air Force to go with the CIA.

He says he's into real estate and investments now. Has to keep a low profile because he knows things—like what really happened to Kennedy. He didn't really die in Dallas. He died years later, a prisoner in Cuba. For all those years, Castro would visit JFK's cell every day to laugh. And that's just a sample of why this guy has to be careful who he talks to. After awhile he does leave. Has to go feed his dogs. Three Rottweilers.

He hasn't been gone but a few minutes when Ruthie herself in a skimpy tank top and mini skirt stomps onto my porch. Her striped socks are shoved into three-inch platform mules. She tosses her long red waves over her shoulder when she asks if he's been bothering me.

"He told you about Kennedy, I bet. He's so full of shit."

I wonder—if she's in on it, too, then she has to make him out to be a blowhard if he slips.

"And that business about the Air Force birthing him? He never got into any Air Force. His folks—they own a string of stores in West Texas—they told him to go sign up since he flunked out of college, but none of the services would take him because of his heart. I know that for a fact. Saw the papers in a file he keeps hidden on the top shelf of his closet."

And I'm thinking, if I'd known about his heart, I'd never have let him carry that bird bath from my car. He has nice biceps for such a short, fortyish man. Shame.

"That jerk," she goes on. "He found a shirt with a flag on it at the D.A.V. one day, added a few little touches of his own, and now he goes off to air shows with the Confederate Air Force. They're too smart to fall for his shit, so I guess they just keep him around for laughs. And support? Fat chance. I make some money at the bar, and his folks—well, they chip in. His sister's a big executive in a penthouse office in downtown Dallas. Plush Persian rugs on polished wood floors with big hunting prints on the walls. She's a Fly Baita Hoop-de-do. It makes him crazy sometimes. She's even taller than he is. That really gives him fits."

I can see Ruthie's real wound up. She wants to tell me things she wouldn't tell her own mama, like what a ridiculous figure he cuts in bed. And how he takes the checks from his sister and buys guns. I definitely don't want to know any of this.

I don't see either of them again for a few days. I don't know if Ruthie's there or not. Or him, for that matter. They are neat people. Not in the sense that I might like them. But he keeps the yard cut and trimmed, and they put their cars in the garage. They let the Rottweilers stay in the house, so I don't hear anything. If I don't happen to see the guy coming or going, how can I know if he is in or out? I don't want that much to do with them anyway. I'm just as glad they've chosen not to involve me in their lives.

This morning the paper says someone set a bomb in a high rise in downtown Dallas. I'm thinking how glad I am that I don't get into the city any more, what with all that meanness going on. I'm wondering wouldn't it be a coincidence if that bomb was in my neighbor's sister's building? Out of all the buildings in Dallas. Silly idea.

I put the paper on the stack to be recycled. Put crime and bombs and meanness out of my mind, I tell myself. All I want now is peace and to be as good a person as possible. But that is not to be.

Around ten a.m. these two guys in suits show up at my door. They're not young enough to be Mormon missionaries. Plus, if they are, they left their bicycles at home and came in a black Chevy. So when they say they're from the FBI and show me these heavy badges, I believe them. They say they are just checking on people in my neighborhood about something they are not at liberty to discuss.

My conscience is clear, so I invite them in and offer coffee, which they decline. It can't hurt to be on the side of the law if you believe in law and order. One of the men glances next door before he doffs his hat and ducks into the house. He must be six-foot-six, at least. He pulls out a note pad and starts making notes while the other one prowls around the house like a caged tiger. He comes so close to the bric-a-brac shelf that my husband's Japanese vase rattles. I'm thinking if this FBI guy knocks it over and spills my husband's ashes, he'll think I'm hiding dope. But it turns out his only interest is in pulling the drapes aside and looking out my windows.

The tall one with the notepad asks, "Ma'am, can you tell us anything about the activities of your neighbors over the past week?"

"Which neighbors?" I ask, suspecting he's talking about Ruthie and her hubby but not wanting to let on.

"The house just south of you. Any unusual movements over there?"

So. My feelings about the guy next door are justified. He's in trouble with the government. Maybe Ruthie is in on it, too. Probably not, though. Hasn't she left him once? Can they be after him for impersonating an officer in the Confederate Air Force? Is that a subversive organization?

"I haven't seen either of them for the past week," I say.

He scribbles something on his pad. "Just what do you know about them?"

I want to be helpful, but I don't think that what Ruthie said about him being lousy in bed would interest them. "I barely know them," I say. "Just that he collects guns."

Both guys come to attention when I say that.

"Anything else?" the one with the pad asks.

I feel there is something I'm not telling them, but I can't find the thought.

"You might be better off asking someone who knows him better than I do," I say. "He has a sister in a big office building in downtown Dallas. His wife says he hates her, but surely his sister would know more about him than I do." I say I don't know her name, but Ruthie would know. The tall guy scribbles some more and then stuffs his notepad back into his coat pocket.

Shortly after that, those guys go away, and the street fills up with cars, and a whole bunch of guys in suits get out with guns drawn and surround my neighbor's house. Surely nothing I said can have caused all that commotion.

When my neighbor steps out on the porch, still in his pajamas and robe and blinking in the sunlight, he looks confused and scruffy and a little sick. Ruthie is behind him, holding the dogs by their collars and giving the guys with guns what-for. I'm watching from behind the window blind, and I see her glance in my direction with a look that makes my neck prickle.

All I told them was what she told me, but for some reason I feel ashamed. It's hard to be a good person when you don't know what's going on.

As they lead him away in handcuffs, I remember what it is that I neglected to tell the guys with the badges. I want to run down the street, waving for the parade of cars to stop and for those guys to get out and listen to what I forgot to tell them. It is this. My neighbor carried my heavy bird bath to the back yard for me, even though he has a bad heart.

Nancy Jones Castilla   *Irving*

NEW WIDOWER

When all of Mr. Flood's friends
And loved ones had died
Or moved away,
A bottle kept him company,
A song and the moon.

But Daddy never drank-
Didn't favor the taste-
And he was "too old"
To begin new habits
After Mother died.

And while he was nursing her
Through Death's long siege,
The domino hall, dust-laden
(Where he'd escaped each day
Before she grew too frail to desert),

Caved in upon itself, shrank,
Like the feeble men who filled it,
Hunched in metal chairs around the room,
Wagering nickels and dimes
In their dim afternoons.

"Ten tables they used to have-
Now only one or two."
So he doesn't go there much anymore:
"'Most everybody's dead
That used to play."

And the widows, who've outlived the men,
Like hens eyeing a new rooster,
Circle, pecking at motes,
Cluck sympathy in the dusk,
Wait for sunrise-and offer pies.

Lilla B. Barnes   *Belton*

GIFTS FROM UP-RIVER

Four old brothers lived right down there on the rocky bank below the dam. Of course, it was just a river then, long before the lake was here. Never a woman in the house, not since the mother died. Just those four, unless you count the hound that lolled beneath the porch or slipped through the torn screen to steal a piece of cornbread when no one was watching.

Papa was tax assessor for the county, and he called on the Scott brothers when he made his rounds electioneering. They gave Papa fruit—jaybird-pecked peaches and mustang grapes off the wild vines that draped the trees and fences down their lane. They loaded him down with tomatoes and fresh young field corn, unless an unusual summer rain made the river come down a rise and flooded the patch. In the fall, when cottonwood leaves floated down the river like little golden boats and frost cracked open the pecan hulls, they'd thrash the big trees in the bottoms with long cane poles and share the gathered nuts with Papa, as well as with the squirrels and crows. After the first blue norther howled down the Leon through the Tennessee Valley, the brothers would butcher a hog. Papa always brought a big package of fresh sausage home. He'd lay it on the scrubbed wooden kitchen table and unwrap it from its brown wrapper. There it would lie, a mound of white blobs of hog fat, pink meat, black specks of seasoning.

For supper that night, Momma would open a big mason jar of bright red tomatoes and another of home-canned corn, served steaming, with salt and pepper and thick cream, the way Papa liked it. There'd be tall, buttery biscuits, and it would be hard to choose between the rosy peach preserves and the purple grape jelly. If anyone could hold another bite after that, Momma would slice the sticky molasses pie topped with crunchy toasted pecans. All this bountiful feast, thanks to God and the Scott brothers.

The sausage, though, never made it to our board. *Four old men living alone couldn't be all that clean*, Momma said.

Donna Buchanan Cook   *Alpine*

CHANGING HATS

This guy walked right up to me and said, "Don't I know you?"

And I said, "I hope not."

And he said, "Yeah, I know you."

So, I said, "Okay" and walked off.

It's funny isn't it? He thinks he knows me and I tell him okay and walk off and he just stands there. I wish I could get my son to do that. Just tell him something like, "Be in by midnight." and then he would just say, "Okay." But I'd like to be the one who walks off. It never works that way. Who can tell kids anything? I mean really, who can? He'd say okay, but then he wouldn't do it.

Husbands don't listen, either.

One time I told my sister Darlene, "Darlene, I'm just going to leave that bastard." And Darlene, said, "You can't just leave that bastard." So, I asked her, "Why?" and she didn't know. She just said, "I don't know." I figured if I wanted to leave the bastard, I could leave and if she couldn't tell me why not to—then I win the argument—the argument about just leaving, not the one about whether I should leave. It's always something with me and Darlene.

She got married when she was 16. She wasn't pregnant or anything. She just ran off with Bud and got married. I thought Momma was going to shit a brick. Daddy just said, "Some girls ought to get married young." I guess he understood Darlene. After that I was told to be home by eleven on Friday and Saturday nights. I wasn't.

Darlene and Bud are a hoot. They've been going out dancing on Friday night, every Friday night, for nearly 10 years. She wears her red ropers and jeans and Bud schleps along in his work boots and Wranglers. He's not much for standing tall. But he loves Darlene and he loves to polka, so they'll probably stay with it for the long haul.

That husband of mine he's just trash. I can't seem to put him out of my life long enough to get divorced. I know he's got a roving eye, but I haven't nailed him, at it, yet. He's always got an apology for something and I'm always lonely, if you know what I mean. So I let him back in—in more ways than one—if you know what I mean.

Last month I bleached my hair blonde and got my nails painted red. It was my birthday and I thought, what the hell, you only live once—unless your momma's a Baptist and then when you die, they let you live again—in heaven. Well, what I was getting to was that it was my birthday and I felt old and I thought new hair and nails might back me up some. It didn't work. I looked like some two-bit floozy. But the deed was done so I just pretended I loved it.

Darlene said, "You look like a two-bit floozy." I told her I knew she'd recognize one and the fight was on. She said I was trying to look like Dolly Parton, but came out like a street-walking Minnie Pearl. I told her, "Minnie

Pearl's dead." She said, "You got it." That Darlene, she can really come back with some good ones.

My kids aren't so bad really. A few weeks ago my boy mentioned going to college. I probably looked hit by a train I was so surprised. He told me how he could work his way through, live at home, and he wouldn't be a burden to his daddy or me. I never thought much about college. He's got me thinking real hard now. No one in my family's ever gone to college.

That campus up there seems like another world, you know. I've thought about going to one of those music things they have sometimes, but I never can get my car to drive up there and park. It kind of scares me, I guess.

He'd probably change a lot after going up there.

It might be a good for him, though.

Then there's me, street-walking Minnie Pearl—not exactly a college boy's mom, I suppose.

One time someone told me that Minnie Pearl was really smart, but she just didn't let it show when she performed. It must be hard to perform a lot. You know, have to keep up an act and all even if you're nervous or afraid.

I wonder if that college up there helps you not be afraid. I mean, I wonder if there's courses that help you feel better about things—about yourself. Well, I guess my boy has some strong idea about going because he wouldn't just bring it up for no reason. Darlene said that Jo Nell from our home-making class in high school had gone up there and taken a class last year. I probably should call Jo Nell and get the inside information about that college—just for my son, I mean.

By the way, did you know that Minnie Pearl once said that the reason she wore a hat was so people could tell her and Dolly Parton apart?

Joe R. Christopher   *Stephenville*

DOC HOLIDAY AND LOTTIE DENO IN FORT GRIFFIN FLAT

(January 1875)
Tune: any standard ballad measure

A young man, lean with TB, comes
    And plays at five-card stud;
He coughs and drinks, but makes his bets,
    And seldom yet coughs blood.

The buffalo hides are stretched outside;
    The bars are open wide;
The soldiers come and herders too,
    And folly is their guide.

For both the weeks he stays and plays,
    He watches losers wage;
His blue eyes cool, he judges all,
    Like actors on a stage.

One woman there who plays his game,
    In Shaughnassy's saloon,
She plays her cards and counts her chips,
    And mostly she has won.

She deals at faro with élan,
    And she can stack a deck;
That redhead is professional,
    With private skills at beck.

"Hello, Miss Auburn. How are you?
    Your hands with cards are sure.
I have a cousin back in Georgia
    With beauty such as yours."

"Well, Doctor Blond, just how are you?
    You know what all declaim:
I'm not for hire and not for love—
    With cards, just call your game."

"Forgive my words—a politeness meant,
    For I love only death.
With whiskey and with games of skill
    I spend my labored breath."

He draws up a chair and settles down
    To match his skill with hers,
And marks are drawn to join the game
    To pay when any errs.

Phyllis W. Allen   *Fort Worth*

MICAYLA'S GATHERING

Aunt Mildred's back was bent as she vigorously scrubbed out the black pot that would be used to make her stewed corn. Wiping away the sweat from her forehead with the back of her taffy-colored hand she spoke to Micayla, "You miss the whole point of this gathering, Micayla. It isn't just about the dinner. It's about family. This is our way of keeping in touch with the past."

"I know, Aunt Mil, but I just think it would be easier if we used a caterer next year. I've got estimates right here. They'll prepare, serve, and clean up and it won't cost much more than we're spending now. The important thing is we won't have to start scrubbing and cooking a week in advance. Look at the time it saves. More time to talk about the old days," Micayla answered, turning her aunt's nostalgia against her.

Mildred Atkins Patterson stopped her scrubbing and sat the heavy black pot on its short legs. Slowly wiping her hands on the cup towel hanging from her apron, she thought very carefully about what to say to her niece. How could she explain to Micayla that this yearly gathering of their family had started shortly after the Civil War and every generation had faithfully passed it on like a cherished heirloom. Closing her eyes, Mildred started softly re-counting the story to her niece.

***

After the war, Great-Grandpa Gus Thomas, a Civil War veteran and former slave, walked from Virginia back to Texas to find his family. When he got back, his wife, Effie, and his three sons, Gus, Jr., Clayton, and Earl, were not on the Jacobs plantation where he'd left them when he'd joined the Yankee army. Amid the destruction and ruin he found several of the former slaves still there working. They told him that Effie and the boys had left shortly after word came that they were free. They were heading north.

For over two years Gus asked every group of former slaves he met if they'd seen a woman traveling with three boys. He couldn't describe any of the boys. Gus, Jr. was only three, Clayton barely two, Effie and Earl were still on the birthing pallet when he left. But he remembered Effie's beautiful caramel-brown skin, her sparkling amber eyes and her soft clear voice.

It was Artemus Ambrose, a freedman landowner, who had a farm along the Trinity River bottoms near Fort Worth, who provided Gus with the first clues of his family. Artemus had stopped in at the stagecoach inn in West Texas where Gus was working as a blacksmith.

Gus asked, "You right on the way north, ain't you?"

"Yeah, by the river," answered Artemus.

"You must see lots of the folks what's headed away from here. Ever see a woman with yellow green eyes and three boys travelling with folks headed

north?"

A shadow crossed Artemus' face briefly, "Could be Miss Efiela and her boys. She got a right smart of book learning? All the time reading and what not?"

Gus dropped the pail that he was hauling from the well, spilling precious water. Effie had always been reading books she slipped out of Mr. Jacobs' library. Seems when she was growing up with little Miz Jacobs, Miz Jacobs taught her to read. "Sho' sounds like Effie."

Artemus changed the subject, but Gus kept asking questions trying to narrow down exactly where Artemus' place was located.

Less than a month later Gus drew his wages from the stage line and headed toward the place where the Trinity etched its watery boundaries. It took over a month before Gus finally rode into the lane lined with tiny wooden cabins. In the open common area an old woman was stirring an iron pot that contained the noonday meal for the younger people who were working in the fields.

"Mornin, ma'am," Gus said as he dismounted his lather-flecked horse.

The old woman continued to stir the pot without even glancing at Gus.

"Sorry to bother you, but I'm looking for a woman called Effie. May be calling herself Efielia. Got three young'uns—sons," said Gus with his hat in hand and holding the reins of his horse.

Never slowing the stirring of the pot the woman looked up at Gus and said, "Down the end of the lane. Cabin settin' off by itself. Ain't likely to be happy 'bout seein you." She bared her smooth pink gums in what passed for a smile, but instead of welcoming Gus it caused him to shiver in spite of the heat.

The cabins lining the lane were one or two rooms of unpainted weathered pine. Each cabin had a small garden on one side and a few had scrawny chickens picking at the bare yard. At the end of the lane the road curved and dropped slightly. On one side was a pond. Gus led his horse to the pond to drink. Rising from washing his face in the cool water he saw her.

Standing on the porch of a house larger than the others was Effie. Gus recognized her immediately even though she was no longer the girl that he'd left behind.

Her smooth unlined face was framed by thick black braids looped into tight buns. Instead of willow-thin arms and legs, the outline of fuller more shapely curves was etched into the coarse homespun dress.

As Gus walked nearer, Effie turned away from the group of children she had been watching. Her champagne eyes widened as recognition began to sparkle there. Seeing her like that, wisps of her straight black hair blowing in the slight wind, confirmed the rumors that her father was old man Parker, Miz Jacobs' father.

Effie leaned heavily against the porch railing. One hand reached up to pat her hair, the other one went to her chest as if to still her heartbeat.

Gus tipped his hat and made a very low bow, "Mornin', Miz Effie. How you this mornin'?"

The children in the side yard stopped playing. They weren't sure what was happening but they could feel that something was going on. One little boy about six separated himself from the group of children. Climbing over the porch railing, the child buried his face in the folds of Effie's skirt. Shyly he peeped out from the gray haven at the man standing in front of his mama.

"Earl Wayne come out from behind me this minute. You hear me?" Effie said as she sidestepped leaving the taffy-colored child face to face with the stranger.

"Who this, Mama?"

"Who is this?" corrected Effie as she gently pushed the child forward. "This is Mr. Thomas, Mr. Gus Thomas. He's your daddy."

Wide-eyed, the child looked at Gus and then at his mama. Confused, he again disappeared behind his mama's skirts.

"Effie, you look good. I've been looking for you for a long time. Wasn't 'til Mr. Artemus showed up out in West Texas that I had clue where you was. This here boy done growed all up. Wasn't nothin' but a pup when I last seen him," said Gus still trying to get another look at the hidden child.

"Been a long time. I didn't think that I'd see you again this side of Glory, even when Artemus told me about the man he met on his trip. I didn't really believe it was you. Never dreamed you'd come here."

"Where's Gus, Jr. and Clay? They here too?" asked Gus as he looked around at the faces of the children watching him and Effie.

"Gone out on the water wagon. Gus drives and Clay's the water boy."

"Job like that usually reserved for the owner's boys. How your boys get that job?"

Effie looked at a point beyond Gus and sighed deeply. "Gus, I thought when you left that I'd never see you again. I waited on Miz Jacobs' place 'til the rider come told us we was free. After that I still waited. Thinking you might come back once the war over. But then things got so bad and Miz Jacobs' was still thinking she own us, even though the papers say we free. She act like she forgot I could read. I made up my mind to take my children and find the freedom Mr. Lincoln promised. Left Miz Jacobs' place with Big Sam, Martha, Zebediah, and some others looking for our place. Along the way Big Sam got himself hung by some paterollers. Martha and some others decided to go back. Said, 'At least Miz Jacobs always feed us and we ain't go no worries 'bout where to sleep. Somebody always take care of us.' But Zebediah, his wife Annie and their boys, me and mine still kept looking for that freedom we was promised. We stumbled up on Artemus' place and he took us in. Zeb and Annie still here too. Right over there," she said pointing at a cabin that was larger than most on the lane but smaller than the house on whose porch Effie was standing.

"Where you live, Effie?"

"Here," she said, softly at first, then squaring her shoulders she spoke louder, "Right here. Artemus is my husband."

"I'm yo' husband, Effie. Preacher said so when me and you jumped the broom on Miz Jacobs' place."

"That was a slavery marriage. This one is legal. Artemus and I have papers. The State of Texas says he is my husband. He takes care of me and our children. I didn't have nobody to do that before."

"Effie, I had to leave. You know that. You agreed. Tole me to go. Said I wasn't gonna never be free if Miz Jacobs had her way. I didn't want to go. Tole you that night I just wanted to stay and take care of you. Take care of my sons. Didn't want to follow Foster north. I was satisfied."

"You was a slave. Could have been sold away any time Miz Margie Jacobs decide she wanted to. She woulda done it too. She ain't never forgave the fact that her daddy and mine's the same. Could be real mean when she take a notion. She was gonna sell you. I saw the papers."

"Why would she 'a sold me? I was the best worker on the place."

"Cause she saw that you loved me. Saw you work all day in the fields and come home tend the babies. Then you come up to the big house just to walk home with me. Drove her mad. Mr. Jacobs ain't never loved her and didn't try to hide it. Jealousy make folks evil," Effie said simply.

"Why didn't you come with me? I begged you."

"I couldn't. I had the babies. Just birthed Earl. Couldn't take them and wouldn't leave them. I knew the only chance you had was to go without me."

"So what we do now?"

"I'm having Artemus' child," said Effie patting her thickening waist.

* * *

Mildred stopped talking at that point. She was measuring butter, salt, sugar, and flour into the black pot.

Micayla couldn't believe her aunt cut the story off just like that, "Why did you stop, Aunt Mil? What happened? What does that have to do with the family gathering?"

Mildred hung the heavy pot on the fire-blackened hook. At the same time her sister, Jeria, approached with one of her secret-recipe caramel cakes, "What are you two talking about? Micayla trying to convince you to let her caterers cook for next year's gathering?"

"Aunt Jeri, what do you know about Grandpa Gus and Grandma Effie? Did they start this gathering? Aunt Mil won't tell what happened after Gus found Effie married to Artemus."

"Mildred, why you telling Micayla that story? Know it ain't yours to tell. Her grandma's supposed to do that. Tell her the story and pass her that bread pudding recipe. Micayla, child, you need to go ask your Grandma Harriet about this.

"You know Harriet is not going to tell this child nothing about the Greats. Absolutely nothing. If she had told the story in the first place the child wouldn't be running round getting on everybody's nerves talking about caterers and such nonsense. You know Harriet has never understood the need for continuing the gathering. She would just as soon we never come back down here. Just comes because it's her duty. Guess Harriet has never really believed in family much," said Mildred as she scraped kernels of corn from the freshly picked ears.

"Grandma Frances always said it was because Henry, Harriet's daddy, left

her mama and married Elizabeth," said Jeria, sticking her finger in the milky kernels of fresh corn, "Needs sugar."

"Keep your fingers out of my food! You know I don't like nobody picking in my food while I'm cooking. That's just plain nasty," Mildred began sprinkling sugar into the milky corn concoction. "You don't think Harriet was going to tell Micayla those 'down south' stories do you? Don't matter to her about family. Ever since her mama took her up north her southern roots haven't counted for much."

"My grandmother told me that she liked the gathering, when she was a child, but then she realized that those stories were just pleasant myths that are told to pass the time. Like she said, 'Who can remember the truth of a hundred and fifty years ago?'" said Micayla sitting down on the arm of the metal lawn rocker that held her Aunt Jeria.

"Your grandmother means well honey," said Jeria patting Micayla's hand.

"Yeah, but she never met Grandpa Gus. I did. He was almost ninety, but was sharp as a straight razor. Told us kids how this land come to be Thomas land," Mildred lowered the heavy iron lid onto the pot.

***

After Gus, Sr. found Effie and his sons he stayed on at Mr. Artemus Ambrose's place. Worked as a hand and did blacksmith work. Gus, Sr. moved in with Mr. Zebediah and Miz Annie. Gus, Sr. didn't talk to Effie much, but he spent a lot of time getting to know his sons. Everywhere he went around Mr. Artemus' place he was followed by either one or all of his sons and their friends. On Gus, Jr's twelfth birthday Effie gave birth to a baby girl who was named Bessie. The boys fell in love with Bessie immediately and as soon as she was able to toddle she too began to follow Gus, Sr. around the farm. The following winter a huge snow came and the livestock were stranded out in a canyon where there was no food. Gus, Sr., Mr. Artemus, and some of the farm hands went out to take food to the cattle. On their way back Mr. Artemus' horse strayed from the trail and plunged down into an underground cavern. Mr. Artemus was killed instantly.

Riding back into the lane with Mr. Artemus' body tied across a horse, Gus, Sr. struggled with the words for Effie. He'd barely mumbled, "Effie, there's been an accident," when the screams started and then she fell lifelessly into his arms.

Days stretched into weeks as Zeb, his wife Annie, and Gus, Sr. took turns caring for Effie and the children. Gus steeled himself against thinking of the fact that another man was the cause of Effie's crippling pain. Days stretched into weeks and months as Effie moved through each day like a zombie. Gus, Sr. divided his time between the domestic duties at Effie's house and the day-to-day operation of the farm.

One day while Gus, Sr. was attempting to explain to Effie about the selling of what was now her cotton crop, he took both of her hands in his, "This has got to stop, Effie. Artemus been gone for almost a year. He ain't comin' back. You alive. Got children who are alive and need you. You got to choose right now.

Either start livin' or you gon' have to die. 'Cause that's the only way you can join him."

Effie's tear-stained face was puffy. Her beautiful champagne eyes were muddy and dull. The caramel skin that Gus, Sr. loved so was mottled and wet with tears, "I'm trying, Gus. I really am. But I just miss him so much. Seems I am always losing the person I love. First you and now Artemus."

"I'm right here. Look at me. I'm right here and ain't goin' nowhere," said Gus, Sr.

"Gus, I don't know what to do. Artemus promised he wouldn't leave me. What do I do now?"

"Don't know, just knows that those young'uns need you. You gon' have to try to get better for their sake."

After that day Effie got better. The boys and Bessie worked around the farm in the cattle barn and in the fields. Effie took over the duties of handling the books. A year later the farm was on a strong financial basis.

"It's time I was on my own. Thank you for helping me. I'm always right here for you and the young'uns," said Gus, Sr. the day he packed his meager belongings on Zeb's mule, Cleopatra. Gus, Sr. had purchased a small farm down the road from Effie.

"What happens now?" asked Effie.

"We do what we been doin'. We takes care of each other."

***

"So then how did Grandpa Gus get the land? Is this his forty-five acres?" asked Micayla. "I don't understand."

"Yeah, well you aren't the only one, child. You never will understand with Jeria telling you the Harlequin romance version of this story," said Mildred taking up the story.

***

"Mama Effie stepped right up and took the reins running that farm. She worked in the fields, cooked, kept the house, and raised her kids. Grandpa Gus was working his place and raising purebred stock. The early 1900s brought money to cattlemen. It was Grandpa Gus who first made the proposal to buy Effie's land so he could expand his ranch. It was huge, but the city has encroached on the original ranch until this is all we have left. Where that new Grapevine Mills Mall is where Uncle Earl's place used to be. Aunt Lucindy lived back up going toward Fort Worth proper. We owned all of this land.

Even though working her farm was hard work, Effie fought the idea of selling her property to Grandpa Gus. It wasn't until the boys came of age and the land fell to them that a portion of the property was sold to Grandpa Gus and the rest divided equally among the boys. At the birth of their first grandchild, the son of Gus, Jr. and his wife Claire, Grandpa Gus and Mama Effie made peace."

"You startin' to be an old woman. Got grands and what not," Gus, Sr., had said to Effie as he sat watching her cradle the tiny baby.

"Yes, I am, old man," Effie had countered placing the snugly wrapped baby into Gus, Sr.'s waiting arms.

"Never thought when I was fightin' them Johnny Reb boys that I'd live to be here with you and the grands. Never knew my daddy. Me and my mama was sold away before I could even walk. Never saw my mama no more after I was nine," Gus, Sr. said, stroking the baby's stomach gently with his large, work-callused finger.

"Yes, well here we are working on our third generation. You know Gus I think it's time," Effie said heading out to the leanto where there were dirty diapers to be washed.

Gus, Sr. had sat idly rocking the baby for a long minute; then understanding caused him to jump abruptly to his feet, "Effie, woman, what you talkin' about?"

"I mean we got more between us than most folks that's been married a lifetime. Now's be time for us to put it together. You been saying that you want to be married and since you don't seem to be able to find another woman willing I might as well take you."

The wedding was held on the following Sunday. Everyone on the lane brought a favorite dish. Gus, Sr. and Effie were married underneath that beautiful oak tree down by the pond that once separated but now bound their property. Every year since that day we've had a family gathering to celebrate Grandpa Gus's and Mama Effie's wedding. But more than that we celebrate our family and how we came to be. The history of this family is carefully guarded and each elder is responsible for passing his or her part of that history on to the next generation. In 1935 when Mama Effie was feeling the weight of her eighty-five years, she pulled her granddaughter onto her lap and shared her most prized recipe for caramel cake and the story of her and Grandpa Gus' life.

"This recipe is only to be passed to your descendents at the family gathering, but only when they are ready."

***

"I started to cry," said Jeria with a faraway look in her eye. "'Nothing to cry about, honey. Your grandma is old. I've buried two husbands and your Uncle Clay. I been dreaming of them waiting for me every night for a while. I know it won't be long now. But you shouldn't be sad. I've lived my life. It was a good one. Promise me that you'll always keep the family gathering alive. Our children need to know who they are. They need to know the sacrifices that were made for them. That's what this family gathering means. Every time you or one of yours make my cake I'll be smiling down at you from up there,'" she'd told me.

***

"It wasn't but a month later that Mama Effie was dead, buried under a spreading pecan tree between Grandpa Gus and Mr. Artemus. Uncle Clay right on the other side. The next year for the first time Mama and I baked her caramel cake, Mildred made her creamed corn, and Aunt Augusta baked butter rolls, rolled them out right over there," said Jeria pointing to a table laden with snowy covered pans of rising rolls.

"Well, we could still get together and tell the stories without doing all this cooking. A caterer could cook and serve the same menu in an air conditioned hotel and we could all visit without sweating," Micayla said.

"You haven't heard one word that we said. Can a caterer bake Aunt Gussie's butter rolls, or make Cousin Mae's potato salad, or Uncle Clay's barbecue sauce? Can a caterer serve you on dishes that your great-great-greatgrandmother ate from? This meal is about more than food," Mildred said her voice filled with exasperation.

"So how long have you been doing this?" asked Micayla still searching for meaning in what to her was a hopelessly backward tradition crying out for modernization.

"Made my first pot of stewed corn when I was thirty. My grandma, Phoebe Thomas-Armstrong, took me aside and told me how her Grandma Sylvia Thomas passed on the recipe after her second heart attack. Wasn't long after that Grandma's grandmother died. I've been blessed. Grandma Phoebe's been here to taste my corn for the last five years. Says it keeps getting better and better."

"I don't like to cook." said Micayla simply.

"It's your duty, honey. You really don't have a choice. Your grandmother doesn't have any other grands. She's got to give to you what was given to her," said Mildred stirring in the black pot slowly.

"What happens if I don't do it?"

Mildred stopped stirring the corn mixture and stood pointing the wooden spoon at Micayla, "See this spoon? My grandmother's grandmother used this same spoon in this same pot. She made her first pot of corn when she was only twenty. Her grandmother died young. Your own grandmother, bless her. Lord knows she ain't no cook, but she does her best. What will happen if you don't continue the tradition? I don't know, baby. Maybe nothing. But what I do know is that this family is spread to the far corners of the world and this gathering is what keeps us connected. Once those strings are loosened I don't know what will happen," Mildred said staring out at the assembled family members.

There was Clay IV and his boys sweating over the barbecue grill, mopping the chickens, pork shoulders, and slabs of ribs with his grandpa's secret sauce. Jeria and her two daughters were placing beautifully baked cakes of all varieties on a table draped with an ancient flowered tablecloth. Various other aunts, uncles, and cousins were busy making the fixings of a wonderful feast as they swapped stories of the year and years past. The sound of lying and laughter filled the air.

Looking back at Micayla, Mildred continued, "This is our gift to you, Micayla. What you choose to make of it is up to you."

Micayla looked at her aunt's normally smooth, perfectly coiffed pageboy pulled back into an untidy bun with stray Clairol Honey Blond-lightened wisps of hair escaping to frame her sweat-shined brown cheeks. The white caps of her perfectly French-manicured nails were chipped and slightly discolored from the vigorous scrubbing she had given the black iron pot. Micayla remembered the weekend last summer that she'd spent with Aunt Mildred. They'd dined at the best restaurants, caught two Broadway plays, and had Sunday brunch in the Hamptons with a close friend of her aunt's.

This wasn't some slow talking, backward, verb-splitting country girl in a worn housedress and felt house slippers. Aunt Mildred was a Gucci-briefcase-carrying, five-star-restaurant-eating, penthouse-living sophisticated woman of the nineties. Moschino, Vittadini, and Dior were her dressmakers. Her long, eleven-narrow feet were usually elegantly shod in Ferragamo, Gucci, or Manolo Blahnik. But today she was in worn jeans, scuffed loafers, and a worn apron tied around her Paul Burgnon aerobicized waist, working in the heat thirty miles from the closest jar of moisturizer. And she was enjoying it. Something happened to her down here. The past seemed to reach out and pull her willingly back.

"Mildred! You all over there yakking and yakking. In between you had any time to finish that corn? We hungry," Uncle Clay said as he and his grandson, Dariel, sampled yet another rib.

"I don't know how you can be hungry. You already ate a half of that hog," answered Aunt Mildred stirring the corn mixture once again.

It didn't seem to matter what they were in their regular lives—Uncle Clay was a high-powered attorney in Los Angeles—down here they were sons and daughters of the South who were connected by links from the past stronger than change, inconvenience, or assimilation.

Closing her eyes Micayla could feel the bond from those same links. Looking around at all of her family laughing and making ready to share this special meal, Micayla realized that no caterer could capture what she was seeing. Slowly she crumpled the smooth heavy vellum paper that Catering by Raphael had used to submit their bid.

As the crumpled paper blew across the land stained with the footsteps of her family past and present, Micayla understood. The gathering was hers. Deeded to her much the same as this land. Laughing, she stooped to grab up a squirming little niece or cousin.

"Uncle Clay, what's the chance of me getting one of those ribs?"

Winner of the New Texas Poetry Award
given in memory of Dr. Robert H. Woodward by
Dr. Larry and Carol Woodward